Jessie's Story

by Jessie Larman

Previously published by this author
"Carnarvon" Published by Artlook 1980

Copyright © Jessie Larman 2019
First Edition Access Press 2013
Second Edition Carnarvon Art Studio 2019

All rights reserved. This book is copyright. Apart from any fair dealing for the purpose of private study, research, criticism or review, as permitted under the Copyright Act, no part of this book may be reproduced or transmitted in any form or by any means, electronic or mechanical, including photocopying, recording or by any information storage and retrieval systems without written permission from the publisher. Enquiries should be made to the publisher.

Cover design by David Shelton.
Cover photograph from left to right: Nanna Stebbings, (later Tainton), Nanna Davey, Jessie Emily Wyatt, Jessie Mabel Rosina Wyatt, later Larman in 1958.

National Library of Australia

 A catalogue record for this book is available from the National Library of Australia

ISBN: 9780987207555 (paperback)
Distributed in Australia and Overseas by IngramSpark
Publishing Consultants: Pickawoowoo Publishing Group

Introduction

This book was written by me, Jessie Mabel Rosina Larman, nee Wyatt, especially for my children and their families. I believe that they will see a great difference between the childhood I had, to their own childhoods, in this present day. I pray that whoever reads this book, will be blessed in some way by it. Thank you to all who have made this book possible. Jessie.

Jessie Mabel Rosina Wyatt, as a baby

Table of Contents

Chapter		Page Number
1	Colchester, England	1
2	About Elsie's House	13
3	Lexden	21
4	60 Barn Hall Avenue	25
5	Technical College	33
6	Early Illness	40
7	Wivenhoe	51
8	"Gayhurst"	54
9	Brightlingsea	63
10	Alresford	69
11	Australia	75
12	"Greenacres" at Sawyers Valley	77
13	Carnarvon	86
14	Plantation Days	90
15	Forrestdale	103
16	Return to Carnarvon	109
17	Divine Healing	116
18	Family Members	121
19	A Prayer and a Psalm	128

Chapter One

Colchester, England.

I would like to tell you what it was like when I was younger. Well, we were poor, but as children, we didn't know that we were poor, because that was how it was. The hardest part is to know where to begin, so I shall start when I was about five years old. Wait a minute ... it just came to me! I do remember earlier. When we were very young my sister, Jean, and I used to play in our back garden. Sometimes when Mum was taking us out, she would get us ready first. One time, while we were waiting for her in the garden, Jean hit me over the head with an iron rod. Not sure what happened about that but I might as well tell you a couple of other things that have come to mind.

We must have spent quite a lot of time playing in the back garden. There was no front garden for that house, as you can see from the old photograph of Hythe Hill, because it fronted right onto the street. At the back of the houses, gardens all had connecting tall fences, including tall

Hythe Hill and St Leonard's Church, Colchester U.K. The photograph above shows the street where I lived as a child. The fourth door on the right was the front door of our family home, leading into the long hallway with a door off to the right into a large front room where the two windows are. St. Leonard's Church was just up the hill where my sister, Jean, and myself went to Sunday school and were Christened there. Also it was there that I invited Jesus into my life when I was about 5 years old. The photo is reproduced with the kind permission from: The Essex County Newspapers, Colchester, U.K. in association with Colchester Museums, U.K. Extracted from their book: Colchester Then & Now.

gates with hooks or bolts that us children were threatened not to interfere with. However, I remember the boy, Albie, who lived next door and who was quite a lot older than us (about six or seven years old). He would come through the gate to our side, if he thought that his mother wasn't looking. Albie was a bit backward, so we were not allowed to go to his side of the gate to play.

One day, Jean and myself were playing with the snails, putting them on the side of the toilet wall (this was made up of slates of wood), next to that gate where Albie used to come through. The snails were having a race up the wall, leaving their silvery trails behind them. When Albie came in, he pee'd up the wall, washing our snails down. Jean went in crying to Nanna Stebbings (our mother's mother), who came out and sent Albie home, having a word to say to his mother about him staying on their side of the gate.

Another thing that might interest you about us playing in the garden, was the fact that there was a large size chicken run at the far end. Jean and I, when we were very young, used to sit on the earth near this chicken run; we had little buckets and spades that we used to dig for worms and feed them to the chickens, putting them through the chicken wire with our fingers. I remember running in to tell that Jean was eating them instead of giving them to the chickens. That was another good hiding we had, one hiding for Jean for eating the worms and one for me for letting her!

I don't remember much about the gate on the other side of our back garden, except that now and again a boy came in to play. By that gate was a concrete path and some old bricks in a heap around the top of a well; we used to try making brick dust by rubbing two pieces of brick together. When we had enough brick dust, we mixed water with it, then we could paint on the concrete paving slabs on the pathway.

Through the gate in that garden was the air raid shelter that was designated to our household. You couldn't see it as it was underground and just looked like a mound in the garden covered with grass. There were steps leading down to a door that opened into a large concrete room. In the middle of our garden was a patch of tall golden rod plants, we used to hide in or behind when we had been naughty or were playing hide and seek.

Well, back to when I was a five year old. That is when I first remember being ill. I was taken to hospital in Colchester, Essex, England. I am not sure how long I was in there but I do know that if it had not been for the invention of penicillin I would not have recovered from the bronchial pneumonia and pleurisy that ravished my lungs. I was put in a cot in a big ward with lots of other cots containing babies and young children. I was allowed to get up and join in a children's birthday tea party in the ward, when I was getting better. Then I remember being carried off a corporation bus wrapped up in a blanket by my father. He walked me the short distance then to where we lived on Hythe Hill. It was evening and the street lights were on. It would have been about the year 1942, the lamp posts were tall and thin with gaslights at the top of them.

Looking back, I remember at times watching the lamp lighter men from Nanna's bedroom window, walking up one side of Hythe Hill and down the other lighting the lamps with the long pole used to ignite the gasket (gas mantle). The soldiers used to sometimes be singing "Underneath the Arches", "Lili Marleen" or that song, "The Old Lamplighter", as they walked down the street. During the blackouts and the air raids the lamps were put out and all windows had their blackout blinds pulled down. Even if only one chink of light was showing, one of the men on duty used to knock on the door of the householder to make sure that they completely covered the windows to stop the light showing through. This was so that enemy planes couldn't see the town from the air during the night.

Until I was about seven years old, we lived with my grandmother in her house while my father was away, serving as a soldier for England in the war. He was in the bomb disposal unit. I was two years old when the Second World War broke out and eight years old when it finished. Therefore, I didn't know my father very well, until he was demobbed when I was eight.

Before going into the army, Dad worked on one of the farms nearby. For part of his work he drove the milk cart, delivering milk to people's doors. The horse used to stop at each house where milk was needed, without being asked. Nanna or Mum used to take a large jug to the door to be filled up with milk, straight from the milk churns on the back of the cart. No great thought was given to hygiene apart from putting the top back onto the milk churn, with the ladle inside. That was before the time of milk bottles.

After being demobbed, Dad used to take me for a ride as a special treat once in a while after he had finished deliveries, when he was taking the horse and cart back to the dairy. Dad worked back on the farm for a while at Wivenhoe, then went to work at Paxman's, an engineering firm on Hythe Hill, just up the road, not far from where we were living. Anyway back to getting off the bus. When we arrived home, I was taken upstairs to bed and remained there for weeks on end. The doctor and nurse were frequent visitors, my mother and Nanna Stebbings used to take turns washing me and putting bread poultices on my sides around the chest, to help heal the inflammation of the lungs. Also a kaolin poultice when we had the kaolin. Eventually, I started to get better and to help expand the lungs, I was encouraged to sing at the top of my voice as exercise. They used to find me jumping up and down on the double bed, that I shared with Nanna, singing war songs and Sunday school songs.

Yes, we were poor. Nanna Stebbings (Tainton) after she remarried, worked at the fish factory. On Friday nights they were allowed to bring sprats (small fish) home, which we used to cook in a pan on the open fire in the parlour. Like I have already said, the front door of our house opened straight onto the street. Nanna used to sweep the payement every morning in front of the door and the two front room windows. Inside the front door, in the hallway, was a hat stand where coats, hats and umbrella's were put. There was always a policeman's helmet hanging on the hat stand just in view when the door was opened, so that anyone, especially unwanted visitors, would be aware and think twice of making a nuisance of themselves, believing that it could be a police residence. During the war you had to be careful of unknown visitors.

Jessie's father, Ernest Wyatt 2nd left, back row

We had eggs, butter, flour and salt, not sure what else though, bought in by the smugglers who used to frequent the pub over the road from us. The eggs, plus some from our chickens, were pickled in a huge great earthenware pot. Runner beans grown in our garden, were salted in another one. Our family also grew onions (shallots) and I remember we used to sit with a bowl of water at our feet to take the skins off the shallots, which were put into vinegar with spices to make our pickled onions. Jean and I used to help top and tail the runner beans and prepare the shallots. Most of the preparation was done in the parlour.

I remember watching Nanna helping to feed her first husband at the large dining room table in the front room, who was very ill before he died. At the end of the table there was a large family Bible. No one knows what happened to it, which is a shame, as I would love to have it.

On special occasions, when the table was set for visitors, always an extra place was set and someone would read from the Bible, especially I am thinking of Christmas and Easter Day dinners. The radio was listened to in that large front room. We were made to keep quiet to hear the news regarding the war.

Nanna's house, as I have already said, was up hill from the Hythe Quay, where the boats used to come in for loading and unloading. We had the bakers shop at the bottom of the road and an open concrete space next to it where we used to play. Across from our house, and further down the road past the pub, was a sweet shop and a blacksmiths yard where we used to watch the blacksmith beat the horseshoes into shape, although it was supposed to be out of bounds to us children. That side of the road at the bottom, was a grocery shop plus the bus stop. The bus would come down the hill, turn around at the bottom, that then being the first stop before returning to town. We didn't usually have much money for bus fares so used to start walking to town then catch the bus further along, which would have been cheaper. Sometimes we even walked all the way to town to keep our penny so that we could buy something nice.

Nanna Tainton as a young woman

On Monday's my Great Grandmother Nanna and Grandad Davey's church clothes were taken to the 'pawn shop' just across the road up the hill. The money was used to live on until pay day, at the end of the week. Then on Saturday, the Sunday church clothes were brought back from the 'pawn shop' taken home, ironed and pressed ready for Sunday church. Not sure if they went to church every Sunday. My Great Grandmother Nanna Davey, and Granddad Davey were Nanna Tainton's parents. It was our great grandmother that made my sister, Jean, and I a plain cotton blue dress each for Sunday school. I was told that she made them both by hand. When we put them on, they called us the 'Little Princesses'

Great Grandmother Davey in her long black dress, reminded us of Queen Victoria, very regal looking in her wheelchair. Well, they took me to see her at her house in the village of Wivenhoe before she died; she was lying in bed in the front room, which was being used as a bedroom. Nanna Tainton was looking after her as it would have been too hard to keep going up the narrow staircase to the normal bedroom. Great Grandmother Davey (Nanna Davey) held my hands and cried as I tried to back away, as any young child would while she was saying it would be the last time that she would see me (and yes, it was). Nanna Davey died soon afterwards. Her coffin was laid out on the table in the front room of her house.

Jessie Emily Stebbings (Jessie's mum) aged 15 years

The front room was only used for special occasions, years ago. It was appropriate to use the room for this and we had to walk all around the coffin to pay our last respects. It was the first time that I had seen a dead body, I was about eight years old. This is something that is not done now, in this day and age. However, I think it is a good thing to do, so that children learn more about life and what happens when someone dies. Previously, before she died, we used to visit sometimes on a Sunday afternoon. In the winter months Nanna and Great Grandad Davey (who died first) used to be found sitting around the black leaded fireplace in their kitchen. Great Grandmother Davey had two lapdogs that used to hide under her long black skirt. Whenever we used to visit they always had the kettle on the top of the fireplace, which also incorporated an oven to cook in at one side of the fire. They were very proud of their fireplace and used to black-lead it and clean it almost every day.

My aunt, (Auntie Elsie I will describe her later), encouraged me to talk to Jesus, to pray and to be a good girl and not to cry. Toys and books were hard to come by during the war years, everyone had ration books with coupons in to use for whatever they needed to buy.

Looking back, I remember that I spent weeks in bed recovering from the pneumonia and pleurisy that ravished my lungs. While there, Auntie Elsie bought me a beautiful big book, which was kept in it's box in the wardrobe and brought out by her when she visited me so that I could have her read a story to me; also she would help teach me to read. Then she would leave me with it while she went downstairs for a while to have a cup of tea with my mother and Nanna. However, afterwards she would come back up, take the book off of me, then put it safely in its box back in the wardrobe with instructions for me not to touch it until she came again. It was a lovely book with coloured pictures, very special, as it was the only one we had like it.

The other book I remember having was called "Sunday Afternoons with Mamma", which was about Jesus. A neighbour further down the street gave it to me second hand, when I was about six or seven years old. I still have it today.

They had to keep me warm because I was very prone to colds. Then I developed a permanent cough, which necessitated being rubbed with camphorated oil on my back and front of my chest each night before going to bed in the winter months. Baths took place about once a week in front of the fire in the parlour. My sister, Jean, eighteen months younger than me, would argue as to who went in first as we had to share the same bath water. Just because I was the oldest, didn't mean that I went in first each time as she was very good at getting her own way, with good loud crying. The tin bath was brought in from outside and filled with water that was heated in a kettle and saucepans on the gas stove in the kitchen, which was across the hall. We were washed and scrubbed, hair washed and then wrapped in a towel to be dried by Mum or Nanna. Auntie Elsie would take care of drying me and my hair, then rubbing the oil on my chest, when she was home on leave.

By the way, we had no electric lights as there was no electricity laid on to the houses in our street. However, we were one of the first families in the street to have real gas lights, fitted indoors, high up on the walls. We had two in the front room and one on each side of the mantle piece above the fireplace. The same in the parlour, which was the main living room for eating, sitting, bathing. We also had one in each of the two double bedrooms. We used 'tilley' lamps (very nice ones) and night lights (candles) before gas lamps were installed in the houses in our street.

One night when I was about four and half years old after Nanna had settled me into her big bed, she went downstairs leaving the night light (candle) on for me. Before I went to sleep, Auntie Glady, a lovely young auntie, came to the bedroom doorway to say 'Goodnight' so I said goodnight, turned over and went to sleep. In the morning when we were getting up I asked Nanna where was Auntie Glady? I thought she had slept there because she had her nightdress on when she came to say 'Goodnight' to me. When questioned about her, I said "she stood in the doorway in her nightie to say 'Goodnight' before I went to sleep". After a few more questions Mum and Nanna cried, knowing that it must have been her Spirit that I saw - (my first one). Yes, she had died leaving Uncle Mick, her husband, with two young boys to care for. They were my cousins, Bobby and Ronnie. Uncle Mick was distraught, as she had been a beautiful wife and a good mother to their children.

Sunday afternoons were not the same after that with Uncle Mick crying and playing the spoons while the family gathered for the usual singing session. It was strange to see him crying as he was a sturdy chap, a hard worker. He worked down the Hythe at the water distillery plant. I don't remember the funeral at all. What I do recall is that, after a few weeks, he could not manage going to work and organising the children to be looked after, so he had to get a live-in house keeper. (Well that is another story)!

Jessie and her sister, Jean

At the age of six or seven I had my own bedroom. There was no gas light put into that room; it was just a small room near the top of the stairs with just enough room for a bed and side table. Nanna or my mother used to take me up the dark stairs to bed; it was very frightening walking up the staircase with the adult carrying a little kerosene lamp or candle. Often I used to think that I could see a great big dark monster standing at the top of the stairs. They told me that it would go away when the light shone on it, as it was only a shadow. But it was very real to me at the time and sometimes seemed quite an ordeal being put to bed and left alone in the bedroom with a night-light, the candle, standing in a saucer of water, which always had to be blown out, when the adults went to bed. It was very frightening watching the shadows on the walls as they moved about by the flickering of the candle flame while listening for the scurrying of rats in the roof and walls of the big old house. Sometimes the wind would be whistling around the chimney pots up and down the street, I used to like listening to the wind. I remember there was a secret door in that room that had been locked and wallpapered over, which led into the house next door. It was a bit scary to think that someone may be able to open it from the other side, even though I was told that they could not do that. When it was built it had been one big house. Apparently, years before it had incorporated the old post office.

While we lived there, the family next door used the old post office room as a workshop for mending bicycles and other odd things. As you came through our front door into the hall, on the left, there was a door to the old post office, that was mainly kept locked from our side to stop people coming into the house. In the shop there was a small staircase, which led down into some sort of small room that had the floor covered with sand, where we children had to hide and keep quiet when the soldiers were searching the houses, during the war years. We could hear their feet as they walked along our hallway. The soldiers were searching for Germans.

In the front room, we had a double storey type of air raid shelter made out of metal, that we all had to get into if there was no time to go to the dug out air raid shelter. With blankets and pillows, we could sleep in this metal shelter. Looking back it may not have served much protection if the house had been hit by bombs, but it was the best that could be done. When the siren went, every one was supposed to go to their allocated shelter, ours was in the next door garden. You had to go down steps into ours; it was quite roomy with seating all around the walls. Oh! I think I told you that. Never mind eh!

We took blankets and pillows or cushions as lots of people sat on the floor. It was below ground, the top part was covered with earth, grass making it part of the garden. The grown-ups used to sit, sing songs, talk or recite poetry, while we waited for the all-clear siren to sound. I believe we had torches, 'tilley' lamps plus candles in the shelter. Someone would play the mouth organ, spoons or comb and paper to make music for us to sing to.

One thing you never forget is the sound of the 'Doodle Bugs'. If a war film is on it brings back the sound in your memory. When they stopped making the noise you knew they had deployed their bombs and you waited to hear if the explosion was near. After one of the air raids, someone found a German soldier had parachuted down from his plane; he was caught up a tree in our church yard on Hythe Hill. He was captured and surprise, surprise, he did not have any parachute with him when he was detained. However, over the next few weeks everyone in the street was given a large piece of silk material and no-one was able to tell where it came from…...it was a mystery. It was excellent silk to make underwear or blouse's. I never knew what happened to the soldier. He would have been taken to the barracks in Colchester. I should have mentioned that Colchester was and still is a garrison town, so we were used to seeing our own soldiers around town or marching about. Colchester is the oldest recorded Roman town and used to be surrounded by the Roman wall, part of which is still there and preserved to this day. The Roman castle is in the beautiful Castle Park right in the town itself. (Maybe I can tell you a bit more about that later on).

Well, apart from being a frail child I believe I led a normal life, starting school when I was four and a half years old. A neighbours' daughter used to walk me to Wilson Marriage Primary School; it must have taken about fifteen minutes to half an hour each way. On my first day at school, during the morning, we were given a small bottle of milk each (1/3rd of a pint) with a round cardboard top that we had to push in before drinking. When I pushed the top of mine into the bottle, it splashed out all onto my blue Sunday school best dress that I had worn to go school in. So that was not the worlds best start to my school days. Then after lunch we all had to lie down on a rolled out mat to have a sleep on the floor. I did not remember having a sleep after lunch at home, so it was quite odd to lie on a mat in a great big classroom with lots of other children.

I used to like reading and used to read walking home from school. The main reason I remember this is because, walking home one day, I walked into the corner side of a concrete air raid shelter ending up with a lump as big as an egg on my forehead by the time I reached home. There were above ground shelters along the pavements next to the road, especially for people to go into if necessary when the air raid sirens went off if they were out walking. Another time walking along reading a book, I walked into a lamp post, so I found out the hard way, that it was not a good idea to walk along reading!

Walking to school and back, we were not supposed to go through the short cut by the marshes, as it was not really safe. The narrow pathway was edged by stinging nettles which we used to dodge but could rub on a dock leaf to stop the stinging if we brushed against one and got stung by their leaves. One day one of the other children, being a bully, pushed me into the stinging nettles, so I went home in a dreadful state covered in stings with my dock leaves in my hand. I received no sympathy, so was in a lot of trouble for being disobedient, by going along that way through the marshes.

After Wilson Marriage Primary School I went to Kendal Road Junior School. I am not sure what age I was then but would be probably around seven years old and I remember being bullied by a big girl, who often waited to jump out to harass and frighten me after school. She then used to chase me down the road. This went on for some time before she was eventually stopped. Yes, bullying did go on in and out of school all those years ago. I was probably picked on because I was very quiet and shy when I was young.

My Aunt Elsie, who gave me the book (the one that was kept in the wardrobe) was a Corporal in the WRAF. She was quite a big tall commanding woman who looked very important in her uniform. Elsie would stand no nonsense from anyone. Nanna was one of the very few friends that Aunt Elsie had, so she seemed to value Nanna's friendship very much. Aunt Elsie was a chef and started to teach me to cook when I was about four and a half years old. I must have been quite old in the head for a child, as by this time, I could read and knit. It goes to show what children can do if they are not sitting watching television, (we didn't have television then). When she was on leave, I used to stay at her house to keep her company, she would have no other child to stay. Elsie wanted to keep me, because her own baby had died at birth and her husband had died in the war. However, my family would not allow that, so she used to treat me as her own child whenever she had me to stay at her house when she was home on leave.

I must say she was very good to me, so I was blessed, as our family was not well off financially. Elsie, as I have mentioned, lived across the road from our house on Hythe Hill and at that time was not a real auntie just the good friend

Nanna Tainton and Auntie Elsie

of our Nanna. Later she married Nanna's brother (George Davey). Then, of course she belonged to our family and became an official auntie.

I don't remember anything about the wedding, it was probably a Registry Office one, with a party afterwards in our big front room. Uncle George had no fingers, only a thumb on each hand. We never knew why, they just said it was something to do with the war. Years ago they used to keep secrets, children were supposed to be seen and not heard! That meant we were supposed to keep quiet and not ask lots of silly questions about family.

Nanna married Arthur Tainton 9th December, 1944. He had been a soldier in India and was somewhat younger than Nanna. Details taken from the Marriage Certificate state:

> *Arthur Robert Tainton 39 years married Mabel Stebbings 45 years. Witnesses: Clara Clewlow & Christopher Davey (who was known as Uncle Mick).*

They were Nanna's sister and brother. Arthur Tainton became our Step Grandfather but we called him Uncle Arthur and Nanna was to be called Nanna Tainton, instead of Nanna Stebbings.

George Davey

Chapter Two

About Elsie's house.

I remember the house; it had one room downstairs with the bedroom upstairs and then another small staircase taking you to the attic room, which was made into a bedroom for myself. The main room downstairs was comfortable, the kitchen area was over to one corner; with a sewing machine situated under the front window which looked out onto the street, where I was taught to use the sewing machine. I remember Aunt Elsie showing me how to make a satin pyjama case; she must have been a good needle woman.

Opposite across the room from the sewing machine area was the fireplace incorporating a mantel piece over the top of it where photographs were displayed, plus ornaments and knick-knack's. Above the mantel piece gas lamps were fitted, one each side on the walls. In front of the fireplace was the brass fender, which had a brass box each end, the lids on each box were padded to sit on. I was given the task sometimes of cleaning and shining the brass with 'brasso', a fair bit of elbow grease and a soft cloth.

Wood was kept in one box and coal in the other. There were the fancy fire tongs to lift the coal out of the coal box and a long brass poker to poke the fire. She also had a fireguard to put in front when necessary to stop the sparks from jumping out onto the carpet.

During the winter months, my aunt and I used to sit in the comfortable chairs, one each side of the fireplace in the evenings to read our books. I was not allowed to talk while she was reading quietly to herself. It seemed a long time to sit, read my book and to keep quiet. One of the best books that I liked to read was the story of the 'Ugly Duckling'. The reason I liked this book was because someone in the family referred to me as an 'ugly duckling'. This was because my sister, Jean, had beautiful auburn curly hair but mine was straight, making me look very plain. Aunt Elsie found the story of the 'Ugly Duckling', she read it to me and said that I would turn into a beautiful swan when I got older just like the duckling in the story turned into a beautiful swan. It is a shame when adults tell children they are ugly or plain. They seem to forget that children have feelings and may take to heart what is said to them. Anyway, I believe, hopefully, that I grew up to be quite acceptable in appearance.

I used to watch the fire burning and wait for her to say that it was time to make the cocoa and get ready for bed. We used to get into our night clothes in the warmth of the fire before going up to the cold bedrooms with our hot water bottles. Sometimes we had some supper—maybe a piece of cheese and biscuits or a piece of cake with our hot cup of cocoa.

She did a lot of reading especially in bed at night and also before getting up in the mornings, when she was home on leave. I was not allowed to take the books she acquired for me home over the road, where I lived with Mum and Nanna. They were just to read when I stayed at her house. I used to love the little attic bedroom, but was always frightened of the empty large size perfume bottle (probably only six inches high), which sat on top of a chest of drawers. It was shaped like a bulldog with a large round face and was named 'Bonzo'. I was forbidden to touch it in case the thing fell off!

It was in the attic bedroom there, that I remember lying ill with mumps. It was such a surprise for my aunt to come and find me still in bed with my glands all swollen, as I was usually up first, creeping downstairs, so as not to wake her up. She had taught me how to use the gas cooker and make breakfast for her and myself, sometimes a boiled egg or scrambled egg with toast. I could take this up to her with a cup of tea and sit in bed with her to eat it.

In regard to the swollen glands, they had to get the doctor to come and check me out. Years ago, we were fortunate to have a family doctor who would house visit, which was good as most people did not have their own transport, so had to use the corporation buses.

Although Aunt Elsie's house was on the main street it had a fenced in garden that I was encouraged to weed, dig and plant from an early age. The old lady next-door grew the most beautiful tomato plants that you could ever see, with huge great tomatoes on them. When we found out how she managed to grow them to such a size we were quite put off from eating them. My aunt used to accept them from her so as not to offend but one day we saw the lady emptying her chamber pot onto the plants early in the morning, using her urine to grow them, it quite put us off.

The toilets were further up the back, through the laundry. The laundry would intrigue the young women of today. In one corner was a built-in copper (to wash the clothes in) the brick surround was painted white (whitewashed) and underneath at the front was an opening where you put the wood in to light a fire. This was to boil the water in the copper, once you had put in the clothes and linen that needed to be washed, plus soap powder and water. There were no taps above this, so you used the hose or buckets to fill it up. We had no modern day washing machine, also no electricity either, so everything was washed by hand, the white bed linen sheets and pillowcases were boiled in the copper along with all white cotton underwear.

Each time Elsie came back home on leave, we had to hose the laundry and toilets out as they harboured great big spiders, which Elsie was frightened of, so she used to give me a penny or some small coin if I hosed them down or helped her.

At Nanna's house, we had a similar copper in the washhouse, which was what we sometimes called the kitchen and laundry. Ours was inside the house and in the washhouse I remember there being a sink where we all took turns to wash (remember no bathrooms). Next to the sink was the gas stove plus a few cupboards. I mentioned earlier that my sister and I used to have our bath in the parlour. I forgot to say that went for all the family as well; it was a large tin bath big enough for an adult to sit in and had to be filled up with buckets of water plus kettles of hot water like I have already mentioned.

What I was going to say about the washing of clothes was that our family thought they were quite modern, when they acquired a dolly tub, which was used outside. It would probably have been about as big as a forty-four gallon drum with corrugated sides (up and down corrugations). After putting in the clothes, water and soap powder, you had what looked like a three legged stool on a pole with handles sticking out from the sides at the top that you put in and agitated the clothes, not sure how the water got hot for this! I remember a long, long clothes line the length of the garden path, which needed two clothes props to hold it up when it was full of washing. Sometimes I had a small clothes line put up when Nanna and Mum were doing the washing, so that I could use it for my doll's clothes and learn how to peg things out. Wash days were very different then with all the washing and scrubbing that took place, not like today where we are lucky enough to put them in the washing machine and come back later to find them washed, rinsed, spun dry and ready to hang out or put into the clothes dryer!

Another thing that was different in those days was that the carpets had to be taken out and beaten with a broom or carpet beater, we had no vacuum cleaner; only some of the posh houses had those, that is people with money, who could afford to buy them.

Like I said, the war finished when I was eight years old and Jean was six years. The shops gradually started to open up again. When they did open, families still had ration coupons to use, to purchase what they needed, as everyone was entitled to the same amount of produce. So those who had more money could not buy extra to the ration allowance and deprive the less fortunate people. My mother worked as a housemaid in one of the big houses and was privileged to use the vacuum cleaner there. I was able to go with her one time to see the marvellous upright cleaner and allowed to push it along the carpet in the hall way.

As a family, we could only go to the seaside about once a year, that would have been the Sunday school treat. We would get ready the night before to pack our bags with buckets, spades, bathing costumes and towels, then we would be woken up early to be dressed and wait in the front room for the bus to come around the houses to pick us up. Great Grandmother Davey and some of the other adults would be sitting up, asleep while they were waiting.

A couple of times a year however, Aunt Elsie would take me to the seaside on the bus or the steam train, to get the sea air into my lungs. Mainly she would take me to Brightlingsea where we would walk along the beach looking for shells. At one end there was and still is I believe, a small shop where we used to buy an ice cream or have a drink.

When they found that I had developed flat feet it was Elsie who bought the special shoes that I had to wear. I always hated those shoes, no one could see the wedge underneath, but to me they stood out because of the colour. They were maroon with a flap on the front! However, Praise God, He healed my flat feet.

One day after the war, my mother and Nanna came home from shopping, they sat Jean and myself on the big wooden table in the parlour. Then Mum held up a big yellow fruit and asked did we know what it was? Well no, we didn't. She showed us how to peel it and broke it in half for us to see and taste our first - banana! I suppose we must have started to have other treats then, but that is one that really comes to mind.

After the war we had a street party down the bottom of the road on the vacant land next to the bakery. All of the Hythe Hill residents, plus others were there with large trestle tables in long rows loaded with party food. I suppose a lot of it may have been black market food. Union Jack flags were given out for everyone to wave. Children were running around, adults celebrating with music, dancing, laughing and enjoying the fact that eight years of war had come to an end. People were able to go about more freely after those terrible six years of persecution. For us children, we could be taken for longer walks without the fear of air raids. Sometimes I remember Uncle Arthur would take Jean and me for a long walk over the poppy fields; we used to chase each other, fall down, roll in the long grass amidst the wild poppies run and play, then sit and make 'poppy dolls' to take home.

For the 'poppy doll' we would choose a nice big flowering poppy with a long stalk, pick it, then break the stem into three pieces, leaving one long enough for a leg after turning the petals down. The lovely black seed box with the stamens on would be for the head and hair. Then we would wind a blade of grass around the middle of the folded over petals for a belt, push a piece of stalk through for arms, push the other piece of stalk up the body for the other leg. We were very proud of our 'poppy dollies' taking care not to break them up as we walked home to show them off to Mum and Nanna, who never came with us for these outings.

Other times, if the daisy's were in bloom, we would sit on the grass making daisy chains to put around our necks as a necklace. As with most children we used to pull the petals off other daisy's saying the words; "He loves me, he loves me not", hoping that the last petal would be the one that said; "He loves me". Not to be outdone if it didn't, we would then start again with another daisy. Then there were the buttercups, beautiful shiny petals a lovely butter colour, which we used to hold up under out necks, for whatever reason now I have no idea.

Most times Jean would have a dreadful nose bleed when we arrived back home, she then had to lie on the floor in the long hallway, with a big cold iron door key down her back to stop the bleeding. It must have been the opium in the lovely big poppies. (We didn't know about that then)! Not sure how the key worked, but that is what was done, plus a cold wet flannel was held on her nose.

Thinking of the long hall, I used to sit there near the back door on the floor to undo the knots in the long rabbit nets. I was a very quiet child and happy to sit for ages to undo the knots. Another thing I liked to do was sit up in a corner in the parlour to draw and paint or colour in pictures. Maybe that is why I am still painting today. Sometimes when it was raining, I used to sit and watch the raindrops trickle down on the glass window panes in the parlour, then in the winter months to watch the snowflakes settle on the glass window panes. Every snowflake seemed to have a different pattern.

Jean and I used to help clean the silver cutlery sometimes on the big table, also we were taught how to dust and polish. Jean wasn't too keen to do those things though and used to disappear to play somewhere. One thing that I liked to do was polish the large brass knobs upstairs on the beds and the brass door knobs in the hallway until they shone like gold and you could see your face in them.

I really don't think anyone does some of these things now, times change but it is nice to look back to how things were, so that we can appreciate what we do now. What child now would sit quietly in the evening before going to bed waiting by a mouse hole to catch one for a pet. Well, I did that and we put it in a cage. I was allowed to take it up to the bedroom (out of everyone's way) so was very upset and cried when I woke to find it had gone. It disappeared with a bit of help I believe, as Mum had told me the mouse was vermin.

Another thing I can tell you is that we used to go pea picking and tomato picking. The farmer would come further up the road with a truck to pick up those that would like to go; us children were allowed to go with Uncle Arthur and Nanna. We used to take our food and water for the day and work along side the adults. Early mornings were cold and damp, sometimes due to the rain or heavy dew but by mid morning things used to brighten up. At lunch time, much fun was had in the haystacks. Also all the adults used to sing while picking the tomatoes. My sister, Jean, who was not really keen to carry on with the picking, would pick up a fallen very ripe tomato and throw it over the vines to see who it would hit. She would duck down quickly, so when they looked around they could not see who had thrown it, as the vines were taller than she was. Well, this would go on for sometime until she was found out and had to sit on the side of the picking field until home time, not being allowed to help anymore. Then, because it happened another day, she was banned from going at all.

I was in trouble from Nanna one day at home after singing at the top of my voice an opera song the pickers had been singing with wrong words. Being a child, I had no idea that they meant something rude. I used to like being in the fields picking the produce and later with my mother when she went blackcurrant picking. When picking was finished for the day, we could go back over the rows, gleaning to take some home for cooking and jam making.

It was unheard of in our family, even if they had the money, nor would they have dreamt about buying jars of jam from the shops, or jars of pickle. Anything that could be made at home was made, including cakes and puddings, but bread was brought from the bakery at the bottom of the road. I remember being given the money to go and ask for a nice big brown crusty loaf. I could just see over the high counter and used to hold up my money for the baker, he then would find me a really good one just baked off the tall shelves behind him for me to take home.

While we lived with Nanna, Jean and I belonged to the Girl Guides and Brownies. We used to go to meetings once a week (I think) up the hill to the hall. When it was getting near Christmas one year, the Guide Captain showed us a rag doll that someone had donated to sell. She asked if anyone would like to have it for Christmas, their parents could buy it for them. Well, Mum had promised that Father Christmas would bring me a doll for Christmas, so I asked if I could have it. During the meeting, I was allowed to run home with it to ask if they would buy it for me. Well, first I got into trouble for running home in the dark, and second for bringing home a rag doll, (which I thought was beautiful) but apparently was not. Nanna took me into the parlour; she said that Father Christmas was going to bring me one. I told her that I did not believe in Father Christmas, that adults brought the presents and that our family did not have enough money to buy one at the shops and as this one was not much money I would be happy to have it. Then she said she wanted to show me something in the top of the cupboard. Well, it was the most beautiful big china faced doll in lovely clothing.

Apparently, they had acquired it from somewhere and were saving it for me for Christmas. I asked if there was one for Jean. Nanna said no, they could only get that one. So I asked if I could have the rag doll, which wasn't very big as I just loved it as soon as I saw it and they could give the big doll (it was about the size of a baby) to Jean.

Then she said I was the oldest and should have the big beautiful doll, and that Mum would be very cross if I didn't want it, so I had to take the rag doll back to the Girl Guide hall. But then Nanna agreed and said that if I had it, I could not change my mind on Christmas Day and that was that. So on Christmas day I unwrapped my precious rag doll. I was not at all jealous when Jean taunted me that she had the best one. No-one else that I can remember put up their hand to have the rag doll. I thought I was giving it a good home and was able to knit clothes for it, cuddle and love it.

Maybe it was that Christmas, (I' am not sure) but they bought me a big black celluloid doll, which I called 'Black Susie'. One evening playing dolls, sitting on the mat in front of the fireplace in the parlour, we smelt this dreadful smell of burning. Mum and Nanna were sitting each side of the fire reading and knitting but could not think where the smell was coming from. Then, when we looked, one side of 'Susie's' head had melted, poor thing, causing the awful smell of melting celluloid. Anyway, I seemed to have had her for quite a few years. As you can imagine we did not have much in the way of toys, mainly because they were not available as they are now, secondly we could not have afforded to buy them anyway.

A couple of times coming home from the Girl Guide meetings, we would come around a back street in the dark, where there was a row of houses all attached to each other with the front doors opening straight onto the pavement. We were in a lot of trouble when our parents found out about the game we used to play called 'Knock at the knocker, ring on the bell, kick at the door and run like hell'. We went along and did this on each door – (about half a dozen), then would be gone before the first person opened the door. We were not quite quick enough the last time as someone spotted us, recognized us and dobbed us in to our parents. Yes, we were in big trouble. But we learnt our lesson and never did it again.

In the large front room we had a gramophone, nowadays it would be delegated to a museum. I don't know where it came from, but we had about two large records to play on it. You had to wind the handle to hear the music and, after a while, the words would go slower and slower until you rewound it. 'Red Sails in the Sunset' was my favourite and I would go around singing it, also 'The Bells of St. Mary's'. I liked to whistle, but I was told it was not ladylike, so not a good idea for me to whistle the songs. Nanna said; "A whistling woman and a crowing hen is neither fit for God nor men". So I used to whistle when no-one was about. Can't seem to whistle songs now, must be out of practice or have lost my whistle. I remember Dad used to sing these songs to us and he loved to play them on his mouth organ.

Chapter Three

Lexden

We moved from Hythe Hill, when I was about eight years old to a new house at Lexden - (called a prefab), which was my mothers pride and joy. By this time I had another sister, Jill. This house was on a small housing estate, very close to the cornfields.

This also meant going to a new school, which was at Lexden, in Colchester, Essex. By this time I had already been to two schools - Wilson Marriage Primary then on to Kendal Road Junior both of which seemed to have big classrooms and lots of children. Lexden School was newer and I was much happier there. My sister, Jean, also was enrolled in Lexden School, so we could both go together, I was in charge of getting her there and back safely.

I was already good at reading and in our class. We had rows of desks and the best readers were made to stand in front of a row of pupils, then go from desk to desk to help them with their reading. So I was made to be a leader and had to do this. In my row I remember one boy starting to cry and when the teacher asked him what was the matter he said that I wouldn't kiss him and be his girl friend. We were only about 8 years old, but I stood my ground and said I would not kiss him. It's odd what things we remember! I have now idea now who he was.

Also I used to like poetry, in class we had to memorise little verses so the teacher arranged for me to go with her around the school to recite a special little poem. As I was a very shy child this was quite daunting. The poem was something about a little robin bobbing up and down.

Looking back to those school years at Lexden I remember especially one winter being the worst snow England had had for years, with big snowdrifts, everywhere looking soft and white. I loved to see the snow, all the trees plus fields beautiful and white, like a winter wonderland. As children we didn't know how treacherous underneath the snow could be, when it was freezing into black ice on the roadways or when it was thawing out into puddles of water.

My sister, Jean, and I had to walk quite a long way to the main road down the hill and then up the hill before crossing the main road to catch the bus to school. One particular morning, I remember her falling into a snowdrift and breaking her glasses. While we were waiting, some people came walking along who told us there would be no buses as the weather was too bad. So as no buses came we went home, skating and sliding along on the thick white packed ice and snow that was on the road, both of us receiving a good hiding when we got there. Mainly because of Jean breaking her glasses, then me, for not looking after her properly. No-one would send young children all that way on their own now.

Whilst living at Lexden there are several things I remember such as - riding up and down Sussex Road on my scooter. The sort that you have one foot on and scoot with the other, then put both feet on to sail down the hill. Also that was one way to go into town on errands for my mother into Crouch Street, it was a long way for a child to go. Another way into town was through the cornfield over a style through a field of cattle (which I was quite terrified of if they started to move towards me); only going that way, which was a short cut, if my sister Jean came with me.)

Sometimes we had to take our sister, Jill, in her pushchair and walking her on her reins. We must have taken the best part of half a day to get there and back, Jean and I taking turns to push or let Jill walk on the reins. It would be frowned upon nowadays for such small children to wander around the countryside and go into a busy town on their own like that. I must have been around 8 or 9 years old, Jean about 7 years, Jill around two or three years.

Jessie aged 9 years

On one of these shopping expeditions I remember going into the butchers shop in Crouch Street (one of the best upmarket ones in Colchester at that time), parking the pushchair outside the shop and taking Jean and Jill in with me to buy the meat that was on my shopping list. The posh ladies started asking where was our mother. I suppose we must have looked pretty scruffy by the time we had wandered through the cornfield, got over or through the style and gone through the field of cows. It was all uphill going into town through the cow field, then the way next was past "Jumbo", the town's massive red brick, Victorian water tower, around another couple of road ways into Crouch Street.

In the winter months, when the cows were not there, it was good to take our sledge (toboggan) down on the snow covered slopes especially when our father came with us. He was quite proud of the sledge that he had made and used to take turns sitting on it with us. I never remember my mother coming with us on the sledge or actually playing with us anytime.

The big black English pram that Mum had still been using for my young sister Jill, had false bottoms in it. The middle panel could come out so any child could sit upright and put its legs down the centre, also it was a good place to put shopping under where the child sat. You could use these prams until the child was about 3 years old or more.

Well, I got into a fair bit of bother when my mother went to use the pram and found that I had collected lots and lots of those beautiful big furry caterpillars (about as big as your finger). Yes, I had lifted the middle panel to put them in that compartment inside the pram! I thought they were beautiful.

One of our playthings of the day, at that time, was spinning tops, we used to use coloured chalk to put on top of them, wind the whip around, pull hard and watch the new pattern go round and round. We used to whip the tops along the footpaths on the estate, playing outside for hours on end. I believe we were quite content with simple pleasures - we had no television or computers in those days, so friends and playmates were quite important. We had skipping ropes and played ball games in the streets. Just across from our housing estate where the corn fields were, it was lovely to pick an ear off the wheat or corn and nibble the seeds when they were ripe.

While at Lexden in the prefab I started to have piano lessons. I used to do quite well to start with at the teachers house, which was just around the corner from us. We could not afford a piano for me to practise on, so lessons eventually had to come to an end.

A couple of times I remember Dad taking us fishing over the river that flowed through the Castle Park. We had a bent pin as a hook and a tin with soft bread soaked with milk in it for bait. It was a fair way to walk but we were happy walking and talking with our father, feeling quite grown up with our (probably) bamboo fishing rods having string on them with a bent pin on the end of the string.

We caught a beautiful fish one time, putting it in the bath indoors for a while as we could not bear to eat it; it was so pretty. Then the next day Dad took it back to the river in a jam jar and let it go.

Living in the prefab at Lexden was the first time we had children living near us, just around the corner, who we could be friends with and play in the street. In the complex there were no cars to worry about and we were far away from the busy road. We never went into each others houses though, just played outside.

Mum and Dad were so proud of their new house, the first for them after living with Nanna on Hythe Hill. Floors and windows were cleaned and polished until they shone; we even had a real bathroom for the first time with taps for hot and cold water. That must have been a real blessing for my mother with three small children to look after, also not having to get the tin bath out any more.

Chapter Four

60 Barn Hall Avenue.

But things don't stay the same for-ever and eventually we moved again, this time to a council house in Barn Hall Avenue, Old Heath, which was still in Colchester, Essex. That house had three bedrooms plus an upstairs bathroom with a separate toilet next to it. Downstairs we had a small hallway with the staircase going up from the front door - then to the left was the front room, through the hall to the kitchen and combined laundry room with back door to the outside. The living room was to the left of the kitchen area. I spent a lot of time over the years doing some of the family wash in the big laundry trough, especially babies' nappies.

Mum delivered my brother, Christopher, soon after moving there. My sister, Jill, was seven years old when Mum started a whole new family, with Clive following Christopher, then Cyril, then Jasmine to complete our family of Mum, Dad and seven children.

From that house I started my next school - Canterbury Road Primary, where I made new friends, two of whom I had been keeping in touch with over the years, but one has sadly died. I am God mother to the other friend's daughter, Catherine, who by the time I went back, after living in Australia for fifteen years, had grown into a beautiful young woman.

While I was at Canterbury Road Primary School I used to play netball, often being in matches after school. We used to play ball in the playground nearly every day, two ball and three ball up the walls of the school, also a lot of skipping, individually and often together, using long ropes which we used to run through having one child on each end turning the rope. We had quite a few skipping games; it's a pity that these games aren't played more nowadays to encourage the children with exercise that is fun and not too competitive. Sometimes, we would use our skipping rope to skip home after school, which always seemed to be quicker than walking. We also played hopscotch and other outside games until the bell rang for us to go back in for lessons.

Auntie Elsie was in charge of the school canteen at Canterbury Road School while I was there. They used to have cooked school dinners in the middle of the day in most of the schools then for children who could not get home and back in time for the afternoon school time.

Also while at this school I sat for the 11+ exam. No one seemed to hold out much hope that I would pass, but all of us, who wanted to sit, were given a chance. I joined the Girl Guides with the friends I made at Canterbury Road School; there was Ann, Maureen and Freda. We went once a week, having great fun especially when we found out that sometimes the boy scouts would be there in another part of the building which, of course, we were not supposed to know about! Our Guide Captain was very strict, yet we all loved her, even though we spent a lot of our time being told off.

I remembered our Guide Captain used to have us marching around to music in complicated formations. We used to go out to perform in different places. Also as Girl Guides we did Scottish and Irish dancing. I learnt the sword dance and used to take part wearing my Scottish kilt and hat of course. One year we did a marvellous 'operetta' on stage dressed in Kimono's and other beautiful dress-ups.

Ernest and Jessie Wyatt (Jessie's mum and dad). Taken at Clacton-on-Sea

We were all devastated when our Captain suddenly died. Previous to her dying she had taken us (her troupe) to a Guide Camp in Wales. There we climbed Mount Snowdon, the highest mountain there. Ann (my friend) and myself took each others photos sitting on the summit. A cloud suddenly settled on the mountain and we had to shelter in a building near the summit until it was safe to climb back down. Needless to say the photo of myself did not come out due to the cloud settling. I believe it took about five hours to climb up and five back down, it was a long day as we were taken there and back to the camp site by coach.

Staying at the camp was the first exciting time away from home that many of us had with friends of our own age, mostly young teenagers. Night times were a bit scary sleeping in bunk beds in a converted stable on the farm. Some of the young ones cried themselves to sleep, while others of us laughed our selves silly with jokes and torches that we held under our chins to look like ghosts to frighten each other before collapsing and roaring with laughter, until the Guide Captain came in chastise us.

My friend, Ann, and I used to get the blame for most things even though we really were quite innocent, nevertheless we really had a great time. One thing we did in our free time was to walk up a waterfall in the woods. The main reason for being in trouble was that we were wearing our uniforms and walking and climbing up in our plimsoll's (sand shoes you call them here). When we reached the top you can guess who were on the bridge waiting to tell us off. Yes, Captain and Brown Owl. We were in a lot of trouble then, never mind eh!

While at Canterbury Road School when I had some pocket money, I would sometimes buy a pennyworth of sweets to take home for my brothers and sisters, as the sweet shop was on the way home just across the road from the school. The pocket money I had was: - sixpence from my mother, sixpence from my father, sixpence from Nanna Tainton and sixpence from Auntie Elsie, making two shillings. Every week I had to go to each one, ask them for it and say thank you to them. I used to guard it and use it very sparingly, even trying to save some of it.

Then when I went to my next school at eleven years old I had an increase of another sixpence making it 2/6d. -that is- two shillings and sixpence, which was called half-a-crown. Now that really was not much money. Sometimes after school my friend, Ann, who always had some money, and I used to go around to visit old Nanna Wyatt (who was my father's mother). She lived around by "Jumbo"—the water tower in Colchester. We really visited her so that she would give us a quarter of a sweet coupon to share, if she had one to spare. Nanna Wyatt always kept some home made cakes in a tin, so she would give us one with a drink of water or cordial. We would then go to the sweet shop on North Hill, with Ann's money and my coupon to buy

Uncle Arthur, Nanna Tainton, Jean, Jessie and dog, Trixie

a bar of chocolate to share. We did this about once a week, then we would walk, cycle or catch the bus home.

When I left school at sixteen years old, I still had only the 2/6d per week pocket money. National Saving Books were available in those days and we could purchase 6 d. stamps from school once a week or from the Post Office to stick in our saving books. It would be good for children, if they brought back a similar saving scheme, as I find children really don't know the value of money these days and it would be a really good exercise for them. It would teach them a sense of pride to save for something when they leave school and join the workforce, instead of relying on credit, then forever paying things off. They would then learn that they would have more money in their own pockets if they did not have to pay the high interest that credit cards accrue.

During these years of growing up my health was not too good; mainly coughs, colds, flu also chilblains, which sometimes were really bad. We didn't always have thick shoes or boots to wear, if you don't know what chilblains are, they affect your toes and also can affect your fingers. What happens is that the cold of the snow and frost chaff the toes and cause them to become red, swollen and very sore, sometimes they even bleed. If mine were really bad when I was little, after trying all the ointments to no effect, they used to make me sit with my feet in my own urine, hopefully as a cure. That was a long time ago; I think it would be very difficult to get children nowadays to do something like that. Also I had the usual mumps, chicken pox and sprained ankles.

I sprained my ankle when we lived down the Hythe. It was on one of the roundabouts at the recreation ground. It was a big one that you sit on and moved around with your feet to push it up and down, round and round or bump it sideways! Some bigger children got on and I couldn't get off. They bumped too much and my foot went under me. I managed to walk part of the way home, which made things worse as we had quite a long way to go. My sister, Jean, ran home and came back with the old pushchair. She had great fun pushing me the rest of the way home down the hill at a fast rate, which she thought was a great joke as I was supposed to be the sensible one looking after them. I was in trouble for spraining my ankle and also for not looking what I was doing, as well as being in trouble for not seeing after my two sisters, Jean and Jill.

For most of my childhood, I was wrapped up in warm clothing trying not to catch too many colds, as any infection always went straight to my chest. At last the results came back of the 11+ exams that were taken when in primary school. Surprise, surprise I had passed the written 11+ exam to go to high school (for girls), grammar school (for boys), or technical college (mixed). The technical school was going to have its first intake of eleven year olds and rename that part of the college The Gilberd School. I opted for the technical college so that I could learn a trade ready for when it was time to leave school and start work as a sixteen year old. But first, we had to take the oral exam. Well, to everyone's amazement I did pass the oral entrance exam and went to The Gilberd School, North East Essex Technical College and School of Art in Colchester, Essex, England.

Having passed the 11+ my aunt decided to buy me new a bicycle, so that I could cycle to my new school, as it was too far to walk there and back home. However, when the weather was too bad in the winter months I could catch the corporation bus at the bottom of our road into Colchester, then walk from High Street to the school on North Hill.

The bicycle had to be paid for once a week at a bicycle shop on the way to town. I had to see her each week to collect the money and take it to the bicycle shop. At that time, Auntie Elsie still worked as a chef at Canterbury Road School organizing school dinners. She was quite upset one day because after a few weeks at the beginning of the payments, the man in the shop, told her I had not been paying the instalments on the bike. It was proved I had been paying, as the assistant had to write it in a payment book that I took each week for him to sign. Anyway after that, she insisted that I take her a receipt. So, I would take the receipt and collect the money for the next week's instalment. This worked out alright as that school was on the way home from my new one. Since I had been little, Elsie had been teaching me about the right way to save and to use money. Really she had been a great influence in this area and I am grateful for the way she taught me to save and to use money in a good way.

At 'tech' (as we referred to our school), after two years of normal study, we started our various trade and business courses. I decided on the commercial course. Everyone at 'tech' had to choose their career pathway at the age of thirteen. As an example, I took Math's, Geometry, Algebra, English, English Literature, Scripture, Art, Dressmaking, Domestic Science (that was mainly Cookery), Physics, Biology, Science, Music, History, Geography, P.E. (Physical Education, Sports etc.,) plus the commercial course (to become a secretary).

During the last couple of years there at sports time, I had to sit and watch due to ill health, which was a pity as I had been a good runner and chosen for several events on the sports days. My tennis was not so great, but I did like playing, whereas hockey, I definitely was not keen on especially after receiving a few whacks from the hard hockey ball and hockey sticks. I used to try to keep out of the way, preferring to play back or halfback. One time they put me in as goal keeper but after letting in sixteen for the other side, I was not asked to take that position again. It was very hard to live that one down!

Our sports grounds were a good walk from the school, down North Hill, around the corner then along Sheepen Road. On our way there we were not supposed to cross the road to a sweet shop. Quite a few of us were often in trouble for being late for sport, chewing gum and saying that; "no, we did not go to the shop". Our faces of course told a different story.

For the business course (in those days called a commercial course), I took typing, shorthand, bookkeeping and accounts, along with the other courses. I decided to give up bookkeeping and accounts to concentrate on the other lessons to make up for time lost through illness and non-attendance.

Not being very financial as a family, we had a grant from the government for a school uniform for me. Also I had free school dinners. In England then, you had a proper cooked meal in the middle of the day, which had to be paid for. We sat down in a large dining room or hall to eat it, usually there were two sittings and we queued up with our tickets to go in. So everyone knew us poor children, who had free dinners, because the tickets were a different colour. While us girls were waiting in line for dinner, the headmistress sometimes came along and undid our 'waspies' (tight wide elastic belts around our waists), which were all the fashion and were banned as part of our uniform. We did choose wide bottle green to match our skirts hoping she would not notice, because as teenagers my friends and myself were trying to get very small waists. Well, they were confiscated so we could pick them up after school time before going home.

Although I was made fun of at school I still liked going, as I loved learning different things, but I was a bit of a dreamer and also a giggler. This all got out of hand one year, and instead of being near the top or near the middle of the class in exams, I came almost bottom. My father, especially, was very upset and had a good talk to me saying they would give me another chance to stay there only if I put more effort into my work and stopped playing around. If not, he said that I would have to leave school early and get a job. Being the oldest of six children by this time, I was expected to set an example. So my friend, Ann, and I were separated up during class time. My work improved with no greater effort on my part (so it seemed to me) apart from actually getting it finished on time and handing it in for marking. So the next year I became first girl in our class at exam time. Even the teacher was amazed, which just goes to show what we can do when we get on with things as we are supposed to do. Poor Dad, he was so pleased with that report that he kept it in his wallet and showed his workmates, family and friends whenever he got the chance. You see, years ago it was very difficult for a child from working class parents to get into high or grammar school so this was a great status thing for our family, living as we were, on a council estate in a council house.

Going home from school the bus stopped on the main road, so we had to cross over to Barn Hall Avenue, then walk past all the owner occupied houses before coming on to the council estate. We never mixed with those 'posh' children, as my father called them, until our teenage years. Thank goodness we live in a more classless society now, with people of all walks of life mixing and being more comfortable to talk with each other.

While I was at primary school my father was not very well at times, he was off sick with depression, not working I believe for about three years, so we had very little to live on. He used to go poaching and I remember going with him. We used to go on our bicycles, taking the nets to catch rabbits. He had a poacher's licence to shoot and snare on one of the large farms where he used to work, when he was younger. Sometimes Uncle Arthur was with us. We used to go at night, it took us about half an hour to an hour to cycle there, then we would spread out the long nets in the moonlight, lay in the ditch or flat on the grass, not making a sound waiting for the rabbits to run. Dad would be there with his gun looking out for foxes. I believe the brush (the foxes tail) was worth a few shillings then. We would gather up the nets after awhile, putting the rabbits in special bags or tying them on the bars of the bikes. Or they would put some inside their coats (I don't remember how they fixed them in) making it easier to ride with them. The nets were quite heavy and were tied onto the carrier over the back wheel of the bikes.

When we arrived home they would gut them in the outside toilet and string them up around the top part of the wall to hang. Sometimes, if there were a lot, they would hang them around the walls in the shed. Other times we also had pheasants hanging, ready to be plucked or sold to neighbours. Yes, Dad used to sell the rabbits and pheasants to the neighbours and friends.

We lived quite well then with rabbit stew and dumplings or baked rabbit and baked dumplings with gravy - very nice! (Yes, I can skin, clean, butcher and cook a rabbit).

After a few days when the skins were dried my sister, Jean, and I would walk quite a long way to the rag and bone shop, which was nearer to town. There, the man would give us sixpence for each one. We were allowed to keep sixpence each, the rest of the money we took home to Mum, or used it to buy whatever shopping she had asked us to get, walking the rest of the way to Colchester and catching the bus home with the shopping. This would take us all day by the time we had done this.

While talking about food, you may like to know what happened to Henrietta. Well, we had a chicken run at this house in Barn Hall Avenue at the bottom of the garden. There were only a few chickens and we gave names to our favourite ones. Henrietta was a lovely hen, with soft brown feathers; she would let us pick her up to stoke her and would come to eat out of our hand. But chickens were there not only for the eggs but for the table as well. By the way, Henrietta (we believe it was her) laid one of the biggest eggs on record - it was about the size of an emu egg.

Anyway, one particular day when we had chicken as a treat for dinner, us children were all sitting around the table with our plates and knives and forks waiting for our meal to be served. Mum put the chicken on the table, all beautifully cooked. Dad picked up the platter with it on and said, looking sadly at us "poor Henrietta, it's like eating a friend". Well, all the little faces around, changed from being happy to looking in disbelief at the cooked chicken. Then a couple of tears started to flow and none of us wanted to eat Henrietta. Mum told Dad that he shouldn't tell us things like that. But he said, we had to learn what life was all about and that if we couldn't eat it there would be all the more for him. By the way, he had plucked it and got it ready for the oven, as Mum would never do those sort of things. However, my mother was an excellent cook.

Sometimes I would sit in the shed to help Dad prepare and cook the food for the chickens in a saucepan on the primus stove, which was on the floor. We used to sit on the shed floor and sing songs while we waited for it to cook. We had vegetable peelings, water plus dried grains, wheat, corn and some chicken pellets. Then when it was cooked we used to taste it to make sure it was good for the chickens.

Chapter Five

Technical College:

My schooling began to be interrupted more and more with illness; lots of nose and sinus problems that resulted in the doctors diagnosing a polypous with the need to have my sinus drained. This, I thought, was an awful operation to have, as there was a polyp up each nostril, which had to be cut out.

Being a girl, one worries about having a big nose after the operation, as it is not too good being called names at school. Yes, they called me 'froggy' because I used to cough a lot to clear my throat (i.e. frog in the throat). I used to be very timid and shy when I was younger but with the new friends that I made when I was about nine or ten years old (Ann, Maureen & Freda) I started to be more outgoing and went through a teenage giggling stage which lasted for several years. This must have been a good help in coping with all the ailments I had including some of the nasty names and things that some of the girls bullied me about. I even had two of my front teeth chipped with a flying stone, then my precious Birthday-Christmas new fur gloves were stolen. They were a present to keep my hands warm made out of rabbit fur. I had done nothing to aggravate anyone, I was just pushed around because I came from a council estate.

In November 1949 as a twelve year old suffering with bronchopneumonia developing into double pneumonia and pleurisy I was admitted into the Essex County Hospital, in Colchester. The ambulance took me to casualty. By this time I was running a very high temperature - so high that I heard the doctors telling my parents that I may not last the night. Well, as I lay there I prayed - the whole room seemed to be just like a bright light and I asked God if I could stay in this world and get better so that I could help my mother with the children, as she found it difficult to cope with us all. God answered my prayers and I did recover although it took about three months before I was able to leave hospital to continue my convalescence at home.

In the latter part of my stay in hospital I used to lay and sweat for about an hour before having the injection of penicillin as it had become very painful due to the fact that the nurses found it difficult to find a space on my thighs or buttocks that would bear another pin prick, as they were covered with bruising and needle punctures. It had got so painful that I had to have a blown up rubber ring to sit on to ease the pressure of the bed when I wanted to sit up. I had blanket baths with the oil (turpentine)? plus talcum powder being rubbed into my elbows, bottom and other sore parts that eventuate after weeks of lying in bed.

 One person who came to help with me was a nun. She was very young and dressed always in white. She would roll her sleeves up and wash me so gently all over whilst I lay still in bed i.e. the blanket bath, also she would minister with the oil and talc. But best of all, if I was not too ill or tired, she would stay a few extra minutes and talk to me. I thought that she was like an angel because she was so beautiful. I couldn't understand why she chose to be a nun and not marry to have children. Looking back now I can see that I didn't know The Lord as well in those days as I do now, because, being just thirteen years old is often the time young girls begin to think about boy friends.

 I didn't have a lot of visitors, as Mum and Dad had quite a big family to look after and lived on the other side of town to the hospital. Mum, Dad or Nanna would visit me on the weekends, also maybe one afternoon or evening now and again. Mum didn't like to come very often partly because she didn't like going into hospitals. Also she would never come on her own to see me. We had no car (actually my parents never did get around to driving or owning a car) this meant that anyone visiting had to walk or use the buses. People had to be quite well off to be able to afford a car. It would have taken up to an hour and a half or more to walk there, as it was a long way to the Essex County Hospital in Lexden Road from Old Heath.

 One visitor I do remember was our girl guide captain. She brought me some knitting wool (a dusky pink) enough for me knit myself a cardigan, which I did. I used to do a lot of knitting whenever I was well enough to sit up or else I would draw, colour in or read a book. They used to bring the library trolley around plus another trolley with sweets and newspapers each day.

 I had my thirteenth birthday, which is on Christmas Eve during that stay in hospital. I can still remember that birthday, especially the evening when the nurses and doctors dressed up ready for their Christmas parties came around singing Christmas carols, wishing us a Happy Christmas. The party lights shone when they put out the ward lights, it was lovely. The next morning, when I woke up, there on the bottom of my bed was a Christmas stocking full of gifts. Also there were larger gifts beside my bed. When the nurses came on duty to wash and wake us, they asked when I was going to undo my presents. I said that I would have to wait until my parents or Nanna came because I did not think they could be mine, as we would have had no money in our family to pay for such things. Also my name was not on them. I had looked at some and put them all back in the Christmas stocking. Matron did the rounds and asked the same thing, she said that Father Christmas had brought them. But as I had been helping for years to get the Children's stockings ready at home I knew full well that there was no such person. So she agreed that I should wait until someone from the family visited in the afternoon. My father came and I asked him if they were my presents and he said no, that I would have to give them back because we could never pay for them. Doctor and Matron came to the bed and assured us that they were gifts that had been given to the hospital to be handed out, that I could certainly keep them and take them home. They were the most presents I had ever had for Christmas, there was even some perfume, the other presents of course I have forgotten but I gave them to my father to take home for the family. I kept the perfume to use while in hospital, and probably a couple of other things like the books and a puzzle.

One other thing during my stay there stay was of a man coming in to tune the piano. When he had finished we asked him to play and sing to us, which he did, the whole ward was in tears because of his most beautiful voice and the fact that he told us he would not be able to use the music sheets they offered him, because he was blind.

Ernest George Wyatt and Jessie Emily Stebbings 1937, Jessie Larman's parents

I was in an adult ward right next to the nursery and as I started to get better they would sometimes let one of the little ones from the nursery play on my bed. I got quite attached to one little fair-haired girl so felt quite sad when she went home; her name was Elizabeth. Mainly in the evenings, when I could get out of bed I was allowed to go into the nursery to talk or sing to the babies and infants to comfort them, or to just sit quietly next to the cots where some of them were bandaged with their limbs tied to the rails so as not to scratch themselves. It was very sad to see them like that and sit in the dim lighted room to sing them a lullaby waiting for them to go to sleep.

Then I had a relapse - double bronchial pneumonia and pleurisy in my lungs. At one stage I just used to lay there, as there seemed nothing more they could do for me, except the injections and pills. At that time no one thought I would survive. I could not stand or walk without assistance. I lost weight and got down to about six stone; this was found out when they had a change of nursing staff. The new sister was so upset by my condition and determined if possible to get me better. As I hadn't been out of bed for weeks and couldn't stand up on my own to walk, two nurses carried me and held me on the scales. It seemed that they also thought I would not survive.

I heard that one young person who was dying asked if he could have a white coffin when he died, so I asked my father if I could have one as well. We always tried to be honest in our family so Dad said he would do his best but I must remember that with all the family to feed there may not be enough money but he promised to get one if he could. Also he said that he didn't want me to die and hoped and prayed that I would get better. Anyway I asked Nanna Tainton the same question when she visited, and she said she would help Dad to find one. Sometimes she would bring me in a cooked rabbit leg to try to encourage me to eat something. It was good that she came, as it was such a long way for her to come. I really looked forward to having visitors.

Most of the time I used to lay half out of the bed curled up with my head in the locker that was by my bedside. Nurses used to extricate me from it then lay me back on the pillows until such time as I seemed to curl up again in the foetal position for comfort. Even at that age I always felt the peace of The Lord with me and had no fear of dying.

When the cough got very bad they used to give me special medicine to stop me coughing, it was syrup that coated the throat at night so that I could get some sleep and stop disturbing the other patients. It was quite a big 'L' shaped ward which held around twenty to thirty patients. Most visitors at one stage had to pass my bed, some would say 'Hello' or stop for a minute. One man who came in the evenings gave me a lovely little black doll for a present; he used to stop to say 'Hello', most times on his way past to visit his sick wife. He said he felt sorry for me as visiting time came and went because I often had no visitors during the evening visiting time.

Well, while I was in this dreadful state I was also waiting to have the polyps in my nose operated on but the lungs were so bad that the doctors didn't think my body would stand the anaesthetic. They didn't give me much chance of surviving anyway and they wondered about taking a chance on the operation, but thought if it was successful maybe I would start to eat. You see I was coughing up about half a jam jar of sputum each day and my sinuses were blocked as well; I used lots of tissues or handkerchiefs constantly day and night. Well, they did operate on my nose, taking out the polyps and cleaned out my sinus cavities, which helped considerably with my breathing and, yes, I did get a sense of smell back, also an appetite that I had not had for a long, long time. I was given morphine to help bear the pain I suffered after the operation.

When I was able to stand up and walk once more I was allowed to move around the ward, talk to the other patients and sometimes help, by reading to a lady who was blind. Most patients had sputum mugs on their lockers as did myself, but you just got used to these things especially when you have been in there for three months....twelve weeks in hospital is a long time when you are a thirteen year old. Eventually, I made a good recovery after I had started to eat, then was allowed home to convalesce. So, I got better and went back to school.

It was not long however, before I developed trouble in my left ear and the hospital allowed the students to try to syringe my ear. It seems that the instruments damaged the inside and infection set in which resulted in a mastoid ear. This then had to be lanced from the inside and I spent about six weeks at home in bed hovering once again between life and death. My parents made the front room into a bedroom for me to save them running up and downstairs. The room had to be in constant semi darkness for about six weeks as I couldn't bear the light and could only lie on the right side of my head. The ear was too painful for anyone to touch it. One night I cried all night calling for my parents who were in the bedroom directly above me, no one came until Dad got up for work in the morning. He put his head in the door to say 'Hello' and could hardly believe his eyes when he saw my swollen face from crying and the pain.

The doctors used to house visit in those days, which was a blessing because most families had no means of transport apart from the buses or to call the ambulance in emergencies. The doctor came and was horrified at the state I was in because the medication, apparently, was not working. Eventually the doctor had to resort to a new sort of antibiotic brought in for me in the form of capsules, which he said was my last resort. They were very difficult to take and the smell of them made me feel nauseous as I put one in my mouth. But the doctor explained there was nothing else that he could give me, as by this time I had had so much penicillin over the years I was allergic to it. I did get over this of course, but it left me partly deaf in the left ear, losing approximately 76% of the high notes plus a hole in the eardrum.

While at technical college I opted to learn to play the violin but with all this ear trouble, gave up because that would have been my listening ear next to the violin and you really need to hear those high notes. Never mind eh! My father was upset because he had gone to a lot of trouble to purchase a violin, which I really did love. It was a beautiful dark mahogany colour, when I used to stand in the kitchen practicing, most of the family did not appreciate my screeching away on it. They said that it sounded like a cat in pain.

I used to go to physiotherapy a couple of time a week during school time for my lungs, to be tipped and drained and clapped on the back. Oh! Forgot to tell you, for quite a few years I had to sleep with the foot of the bed raised to help drain my lungs. Most of the time my sister was sleeping in the double bed with me so she was not very happy having to sleep partly upside down.

I cannot forget having congestion of the lungs and was at home in bed for a long time. The neighbours used to visit me and wondered how I could keep so cheerful, giving them a smile and looking pleased to see them. It must have been The Lord because they said they always went away feeling better than when they came. They used to sit and tell me their problems and talk about all sorts of things. Mum would make a cuppa and she would come up and sit with us in my bedroom. Often I was full of pain and not being able to talk or move much, they must have found it peaceful just to come and sit there for a while to keep me company. I remember getting better and being able to sit and look through the front windows at the people going to and from work and school. They used to wave to me sometimes and that was how I first met Patrick Larman (who became my husband). He used to wave as he went past on his bike going to and from work as an apprentice plumber.

I was fifteen then. I hadn't been to school for several months nor had I been able to go out anywhere, (remember we didn't have a car and I couldn't walk very well). Pat was quite new to our street so we didn't know each other. One day, there was a party over the green near us and they were going to choose a beauty queen for the festival, so he plucked up courage and came to ask if I would like to go over with him. You see, I was able to sit on a chair on the front door step by this time, to take in the fresh air, read and knit while recovering again at home.

When Pat came, I had to tell him that I couldn't walk, because being in bed for so long and off my feet they had got set sideways, but by now I could stand holding onto things. My mother had bought me a pair of white sandals that she had sent away for from the club book that we used to order from and pay so much a week. It was a real treat for me to have them. While I lay in bed, they strapped my feet into them hoping that it would be an incentive to get me walking again. They had begun to despair if ever I would. I remember on Queen Elizabeth's coronation day, everyone had gone out of the house, it very quiet as my mother had gone to watch the coronation on a neighbour's television. So I strapped the sandals on to my feet, got out of bed, edged myself out of the bedroom on my bottom to the top of the stairs and was about halfway down, going down each step on my bottom, when Nanna appeared at the foot of the stairs and was quiet alarmed seeing me there. When I got to the bottom she helped me through the hallway into the kitchen to sit and listen to the coronation of Queen Elizabeth 11 on the radio, that being the reason and incentive I had needed to come down stairs. It was a turning point in my learning to stand up and walk again.

Chapter Six

Early Illness

Back now to Pat inviting me to go over to the green with him. Well, he helped to sit me on his bicycle then pushed me on it to where most of the teenagers were congregating for the Festival Queen to be chosen. The 'green' is what you call a town oval in Australia. Surprise, surprise I was chosen to be the Festival Queen. The organiser said I would have to ride in a horse and carriage on the day of the Festival. When I told them I couldn't walk, they said they were sorry, but the runner up would have to take my place. There was uproar from a lot of the teenagers and young people because the runner up, who was very pretty with blond hair and lived at the other end of the housing estate, belonged to a rival gang. So their lot cheered her on and our lot boo-ed. It seems so odd to look back and think of these things. To me it was a great boost to my confidence to even have been chosen because while I was growing up they used to call me an ugly duckling, the plain one in the family. So I must have started to blossom when I became a teenager. Praise God I got better again, went back to school and had to leave out a couple of subjects to catch up on all the others.

When I was fifteen years old, still at technical college, because of the cough I had to see a specialist who diagnosed bronchiectasis and advised a lobectomy, that is have the lower lobe of my left lung removed. While I was waiting to see the specialist at the Essex County Hospital in Colchester, I was taken into a small room with a bed and instructed to lay on my back ready to be examined. The specialist was quite busy so as I lay there coughing, they had to bring me something to cough the sputum into, they were quite amazed to find that the quantity expectorated was enough to half fill a one pound jam jar (i.e. 500g jar). After the chest specialist had examined me, I returned home on the bus to find my mother scrubbing the kitchen floor. I told her that the specialist had diagnosed bronchiectasis and that I would have to go to a big London hospital to have a third of my left lung cut off!

At first she didn't believe me of course, until I told her that the doctor would be writing to confirm it. Poor Mum, she dropped the scrubbing brush into the bucket of soapy water, wiped her hands on her pinafore and just didn't know what to say. When my father came home from work he couldn't believe it either and wondered how we would manage because, by then, I was the eldest of five children. My brothers and sisters were Jean, Jill, Christopher and Cyril. Although sickly most of the time and going to school I did help at home with the children. I always loved looking after the children and used to look after Cyril so much that people used to think that he was my child.

My mother and father were both against me having the operation as there was a chance that I would not pull through and survive, as it meant being a long time on the operating table and my lungs were not in very good condition to cope with the anaesthetic. On the other hand, if I did not have the operation, it was most likely that I would not survive another bout of bronchial pneumonia and pleurisy, so therefore may die anyway. By this time, Pat and I were going out together as boy and girl friend so I was able to talk to him as well about it.

Like I mentioned earlier at this stage of my life I used to sleep with the foot of the bed (that I shared with my sister Jean) resting on house bricks to tip it up therefore helping to cough up sputum throughout the night. It was around that time that I thought I would not be a good candidate for marriage. I really thought that I should have the operation in the hope of leading a more normal life. A good support at that time was my headmistress at school, who tried her best to explain about lungs to me. Remember this was a long time ago in the 1950's; people did not seem to have as much knowledge of how the body works in comparison to today's society.

Anyway, we decided that I should have the operation, and I left it with God to sort out. Whilst waiting for the operation, one had to go onto a waiting list for quite a long while in those days. I finished my schooling at sixteen years of age, even though they asked me to stay on for higher education to study art. Being then the eldest of six children, it was necessary for me to leave school and go to work. Mum never went out to work full time but did part time work of cleaning at some firm; also she used to take in ironing, which I did a fair bit of.

At sixteen, I was qualified for secretarial work. While I was still at school my sister, Jean, had already left school and was working, even changing jobs several times. One type of work she had was delivering milk, I remember my art master asking me how I could deliver his milk early in the morning, then get to school on time. He found it very difficult to believe I had a sister who looked very much like me. When not standing next to each other we were often mistaken for the each other. I spent a lot of time being in trouble for what my sister had done, as she was a real tomboy. Then, of course during our teenage years, she had lots of boyfriends and I was the one in bother when people said they saw me in places that I wasn't. I remember I used to stay home and put the children to bed and she would be off out as soon as our mother was out the door in the early evenings. Mum used to put Dad's dinner on a plate over a saucepan of hot water till he came in from work and Jean and I were supposed to take turns to see after the children and get them ready for bed.

When Pat and I started to go out together he would come over for me all dressed up ready for us to go out. Most times, Jean would be gone, so there we were, he used to sit and wait while I got the children to bed, change and feed the baby and wait till Dad came home. Jean had the excuse that as she was working and as I was still at school she was entitled to go out in the evenings; also I had homework to do most nights. While I was busy doing whatever, she would nip upstairs to the wardrobe, sometimes put on some of my good clothes then disappear before I could see her, just shouting that she would be back later, as she was rushing out of the door!

It's a great thing in a family when a child goes to work. When I first found employment we used to joke about it, saying watch out that I don't get the sack the first day. Well I did! It just happened that one of the young women working there was about to go into hospital for an operation. That was why they wanted to train someone to take her place. However, I did not know that, so I said that's funny so am I. The one thing that I should not have said, as they wanted a permanent office worker that could be trained and reliable, not someone who was going to require a long time recuperating after such a traumatic operation involving the lungs. During tea break, she told the boss, who came and asked me if that was the truth, so I was very sad to be sent home after just one morning working there. Everyone was very nice to me but that was that.

My parents were cross that I had lost the job and so was the education department that had found it for me, as work was not easy to find at that particular time. When looking for another position, I was told not to say anything about having an operation. This, I would find very difficult, as it seemed like not telling the truth, also for years I had been going to the doctors and hospital with my ear and was waiting for an operation on that as well at our local hospital.

The employment people then found me a junior position in a larger firm as an invoice typist, receptionist with general office duties. During the interview, I just couldn't be dishonest, so I told them that I was waiting to go into hospital but that I did need the work and hopefully thought that I would be a good worker if they would consider taking me on. So in the light of all this as they were looking for someone honest they said Yes, but would only offer me a low wage. They agreed to keep my job open between operations as long as I was sure that I would to back when I had recovered and they realized I would need time for doctor's appointments and so on. They were very good in that respect, so I accepted the position on a very low wage.

This was a family firm; they only offered a very low wage because, as they pointed out at the interview, no one would want to employ me knowing the condition that I was in. You see I had a permanent cough and also nasal trouble; I had had two operations on my nose, by this time, for polyps. These operations had been performed in my school time. I had lost a lot of schooling, whole terms at a time, but used to catch up with the class, using the bookkeeping/accounts subject time (that I had been allowed to opt out of) to catch up on the other subjects.

It was lovely to have a pay packet however small, to be able to give my mother my keep and to start saving to buy shoes and clothes. Also, I was able to buy sweets or biscuits for the children. One week's wages then was not enough to by a pair of shoes, so for my first pair of high heels I

Jessie aged 18 years

paid so much each week until they were paid for. They were green and I thought they were great.

Pat became my permanent boyfriend when I was fifteen and a half years old; he was six months older than me and was working as an apprentice plumber, while I was still studying at Tech. Mainly we used to go out as a foursome with my girlfriend, Ann, and her boyfriend Paul, who eventually married. I am Godmother to their first daughter Catherine.

Well, where was I? Yes, the lung operation. Eventually the letter came for me to go into Brompton Hospital in London. When they examined me, they found that I still needed the operation on my left ear as it was still causing me a lot of pain and suffering due to the mastoid infection, previously mentioned, which had been lanced, discharging pus for up to six weeks. The left side of my head had been badly affected. They operated on my ear in The Royal Brompton Hospital in London because they said they could not operate on my lung until the ear was healed, as it was in such a mess. It was all very painful, but it had to be done. This is now the year 2013, so this testimony is to let people know that The Lord Jesus healing power is the same today, as it was over 2000 years ago.

Well at the age of eighteen years I had the lung operation - a lobectomy, i.e. the lower lobe of the left lung was cut off. However, the bronchiectasis later spread to my right lung as well. There is no known cure for this illness, which is similar to emphysema, for which there is no known cure either. The operation took place in The Royal Brompton Hospital in London. It was a huge great hospital spanning both sides of Brompton Road, with a tunnel underneath the road where I was wheeled through while in a hospital bed wired up with drip bottles, into the lifts, down one side of the hospital under the tunnel then up to the other part of the hospital on the other side of the road. It was quite an experience being moved by the nurses and wondering where I was going, along the underground passages. It was in that hospital that I was taken to the Sunday services in the beautiful little Chapel. The Christmas that I was there, as I lay in bed listening to the Hallelujah Chorus on the radio headphones, a kind nurse came to cry with me because she was so sad at being away from home and her family for Christmas.

In regard to the operation, the doctors asked if they could try a new way of stitching me up after the operation. It was said to work well in theory, although for myself I could not see how it would work in practice, but I said yes, I would give it a go. I had already been used as a guinea-pig for some huge great tablets (hoping for a cure), which turned out not to be any good for my condition, but was worth a try just in case it would save me having the operation.

Well, I had thirty-nine stitches around the back and left side of my chest, stitched up by their new theory method i.e. oversewn with one long thread, which they hoped would pull out in one piece. What happened, of course, after ten days healing of the incision, the blood and skin that was growing around the thread, obviously tightened where the needle holes were! So when the time came to take out this long thread, they cut the knot at one end, pulled on the other and nothing happened. By the way they did spray me with local anaesthetic, so I would not feel much pain. Anyway, the thread was well and truly embedded in the skin, so they had to cut each oversew of the stitches then pull them out individually, which was much better because the thread itself had hardened and was all a dark colour from the blood.

However, it left a very good neat scar and was a better way to stitch up than tying individual stitches into knots that would have pricked into the skin. So all was well except we learnt the lesson that what seems all right in theory will not always workout in practice. I sat and watched the doctor and nurses take them out and saved them for years in an envelope. I may even have them still somewhere…not sure about that!

Jessie and fiancé Pat

Another thing that happened soon after the operation was the lung collapsed. I had to have the fluid taken out, quite a lot, about a pint. It was interesting to watch them draw it off the lung, the doctors and nurses were very good to me, giving me local anaesthetic and propping me up to watch. I always feel better when people explain exactly what they are going to do so that I know what to expect. Most people turn away but it was interesting to watch the fluid being drawn out!

One afternoon while we were waiting for visitors, everything went dark; they put the lights on in the ward, but outside it was just like the blackest of nights. Pat came to visit me that afternoon and told me what had been happening outside. Apparently, suddenly when everything went dark, he said that people were very frightened and some knelt down on to the steps to pray. It was very peculiar; some of the patients and staff were very frightened. I had been busy comforting an upset and very scared young girl, when the emergency lights came on in the ward. I managed to get out of my bed and go over to hers after pressing the bell for the nurse. The humidifier (that was like a large kettle with a long spout) standing on a table next to her bed, in the tent that was covering her bed, was spraying hot water instead of steam, so I was trying to turn it away from her just as the nurse came to help. This had probably happened due to the power being disrupted, interfering with the electricity controlling the steam that should have been coming out of the humidifier. They probably do not use those kind of big humidifiers now. I reassured the child that God would look after us and for her not to be afraid. After that I was back into bed to wait for visiting time.

Then it was good to see Pat during afternoon visiting time. It would have taken him most of the day to get to there from Old Heath Colchester on the bus to town, then the train from North Station to London and change to the underground train to the nearest station for Brompton Hospital then to walk the rest of the way for our visit. Afterward he had to do the same travelling in reverse to get back home, it was obviously a long day.

When I started to get better - Harrods.!!! Well, I must just tell you this. When you are well enough, you are allowed out from hospital as long as someone is with you. I had no family in London, so didn't think there was much chance of me going out around the shops or even out of the hospital, but one of the young nurses was asked to accompany me if I would like to go. Yes, of course I said I would, but we had another problem. I had no clothes to wear, only pyjamas, so one of the other patients, (a teenager from Wales), said that I could borrow her clothes. She was shorter than me, so her coat only came just to my knees and was a bit tight but never mind it would button up, so hopefully, we thought it would look all right. The only thing that I objected to was wearing someone else's knickers......so, I decided to stitch my white silky style pyjama legs up to wear instead of her knickers.

Pat and Jessie

When the day came, the young nurse came in the afternoon to escort me and off we went. It felt very strange wearing someone else's clothes going down in the lift and out into the street, after being in bed so long. We decided to go into Harrods, (the store that the Queen shops in), as it was not too far for us to go. We had a good time looking in the different departments that interested us most. The last department was the bridal one, because Pat and I were engaged to be married, so it was beautiful to look and see all the magnificent dresses and ensembles there. The prices were much more than we could ever even think to afford. In that department they had really large mirrors to reflect the dress exhibits. Looking into one of these we could see ourselves, then suddenly, I was aware that one of my pyjama legs was hanging down below the coat that I was wearing.

Apparently, some of the stitches, I had so quickly sewn to hold the trouser leg up, were coming undone. When we saw this, we started to laugh and were immediately spoken to by a saleswoman, because it was quite unseemly to stand and laugh apparently in that department. I remember it was so quiet and awesome in there with all the mirrors, the mannequins dressed in the most fabulous dresses you could ever hope to see. So, doubling up with laughter we could hardly speak to the saleswoman and we then made a hasty retreat, not only from that department but from the building, as it was difficult trying to hitch up the pyjama leg with my hand in my coat pocket, holding it all the time, as we tried to find our way out of the shop and then back to the hospital. Once outside Harrods we just doubled up again with laughter, which of course is very good therapy. We relayed all this to the hospital ward on our return; it certainly livened up the day for the patients, especially the one from Wales, who I had borrowed the clothes from.

I am not sure how long I was in The Royal Brompton Hospital but from there I went to convalesce at Cobham in Surrey, at The Schiff Home of Recovery. It was a really large place in beautiful grounds; looking out from our windows we could watch the squirrels play and when we were well enough to sit outside, we liked to feed them titbits. While convalescing I was in a huge great ward with the beds quite close together; people of all nationalities were recovering there. Lung patients, amputees, heart patients also others, from all different hospitals throughout England. Bath time started in the very early hours of the morning, only allowing so many minutes for each patient. Years ago, the facilities were very antiquated in the bathroom. We had to have a nurse stay in with us to help us in and out of the bath, until of course, we were able to fend for ourselves. Then we were put back to bed to wait for breakfast. I was still having physiotherapy for my left arm and lungs, everything was very painful. It was good that Pat was able to visit me one day on a weekend having travelled on buses and trains to get there. I was there about three weeks before going home to finish convalescing.

Riding a bike was one of the best therapies to expand my lung and heal the left arm to get it moving again. I took a few years to really come good, at first I had to spray a local anaesthetic on my left side before I could get dressed, as something had happened and left it very sensitive to the touch. Also my thighs were sensitive to the touch for a number of years due to all the injections. Anyway everything healed up beautifully even though I still had a cough i.e. chronic bronchitis but the lungs were a lot better.

Pat and I married on 1st February, 1958, we were both twenty-one years of age, so had been going out together for about five years. In those days, you would not have dreamt about living together unless you were married.

We were married in the Roman Catholic Church called St. James the Less, in Colchester, England. I did not change my religion from Church of England but had to agree to a Roman Catholic wedding, as I did want our wedding to take place in church. Also I had to agree to bring our children up in my husband's faith. I was not happy about that but agreed to have them baptized (assuming that we would have any) in that church.

Pat's father and mother, Pat, Jessie, Jessie's father and mother- wedding day 1st February, 1958

Well, we did have three children, Josephine, Ruth and Matthew. I will tell you about them later, and yes, we did have them baptized into the Roman Catholic religion.

As Pat opted not to continue going to church, I was able to let them come to our Church of

England Sunday School when we later moved to Alresford, because it was then too far for me to take them elsewhere. I hoped they would choose their own church when they would become adults.

My mother was against us getting married, as mixed religious marriages were frowned upon years ago. Both mothers never got on together, choosing not to walk up the same side of the road together or talk to each other, even though they lived almost opposite across the road in Barn Hall Avenue. Years ago, we needed our parents permission to marry, if we were under twenty one years of age. So waiting until the year that I would be twenty one years old, they gave us their permission to marry in 1958.

On the wedding day my mother had to be persuaded to get ready, as she suddenly declared she was not coming, so it was quite a traumatic day getting her ready as well as my bridesmaids. I was happy that I had been able to make our bridesmaids dresses for my sister, Jill, cousin, Sylvia from Coventry and Pat's youngest sister, June. They all looked beautiful. We had pale blue material, with white flock flower design for the two older ones and white printed satin for June who was about 10 years old at the time.

Jessie with her father on her wedding day

The wedding went off very well with family plus friends coming, then on to a lovely reception that was organized by Aunt Elsie in a church hall with some of her chefs and cooks from Elsie's work place.

Then off to our honeymoon at Butlin's Holiday Hotel in Margate. That was a beautiful hotel with a large indoor swimming pool, ballroom, games room and dinning room. Margate is a seaside town, so we had the beach nearby, it was very good.

Pat and Jessie on their wedding day 1958

Chapter Seven

Wivenhoe

When we were first married we lived with Pat's family across the road from mine in Barn Hall Avenue. Pat was in the Army for his National Service when we married. I was working at a firm in Hawkins Road, across the river down the Hythe. It was a timber merchants firm. When I took on this job, they were looking for someone to set up an invoice office. They took me on the train to their Clacton branch to see how things were organized there, so I was able to set up the first office they had in the Colchester branch for invoicing.

I did invoicing mainly, but also some secretarial work. With this work I became very proficient at typing with a good typing speed of well over 100 words per minute on one of those big old heavy typewriters. I really loved office work, even checking out the hundreds of invoices by hand with no calculator! They did have an old comptometer-(adding up machine), which we could use it if we could not agree on the total of an invoice. But we were encouraged not to use the comptometer, as they preferred us to calculate the discounts with paper and pencil, as it was quicker than using the machine.

After about a year living in Pat's family home with his mother, father, sisters, Pam, June and Delia (Pat was still in the Army) on doctors orders regarding myself, we moved to Wivenhoe, to my Aunt Elsie's cafe. Elsie was then married to Uncle George Davey - Nanna Tainton's brother. They were delighted that we wanted to come and live with them in the café and allowed us to have the large room at the top.

So Pat and I lived on the third floor, Elsie and George on the second floor with the café on the ground floor. The café was very pleasant, with a big window each side of the front door. Elsie kept the inside nice with all tables having tablecloths and four chairs around them. It looked very homely and I was quite happy to help in there, especially at weekends and sometimes when I came back from work.

Like I said, we lived on the third floor, which we made into a bed-sit. It had two large windows at the front that looked out onto the village street, where we could see the fish & chip shop and the road way down to the shipyard. We had a fireplace in the room where we used to burn coal and wood to keep warm in the winter months, as it was quite a large room. The dining table and chairs were near the front windows, then a lounge area in the middle of the room. The other end we used with dividing curtains for a bedroom area. There was another large window to look out of at the back of the bedroom. Our staircase went down to the second floor where Elsie and George lived. The second floor consisted of a very large lounge room at the front a hallway with toilet and bathroom, a large bedroom then leading to another large spare bedroom. Their staircase went down to the kitchen and café. The kitchen was great with stainless steel sinks, cooking stoves and everything that was needed. In between the kitchen and café there was another small area with a Rayburn stove plus deep fryer and the counter where people could order.

We used to open on Friday evenings for fish & chips and had people queuing up then, as Elsie was an excellent cook. Uncle George worked at the shipyard as a watchman, also at times, a night-watchman. At weekends, I would now and then walk down to see one of the ships being built then walk along the river bank, sometimes taking a book to sit on the grass and read for a while.

Elsie, Jessie George - Gables Cafe 1960

It was good when Pat came home on leave for a few days from Aldershot where he was stationed during his national service. Sometimes, we would walk along the river bank together or go to visit our families. As we had no car, we walked everywhere or caught the bus or train. Some days we would go across on the ferry (it was a rowing boat) that could hold a few people, plus a couple of bicycles. The ferry boat would go across the river to Rowhedge and back again to Wivenhoe. Once across at Rowhedge, Pat and I could walk through the lane ways to Old Heath to visit our families. In the winter, when daylight saving came to an end, the ferry closed around 4pm as it would start to get too dark to cross over the river. So if anyone was stranded on the other side it would take an hour or two to travel around the town to get home, instead of just about a few minutes across on the ferry.

In the evenings, we quite often went to the Pub for a drink with our friends Thelma and Terry (who lived in the butchers house and shop next door) or with Elsie and George. There was a nice Pub next to the café named 'The Black Buoy', also one just down the road by the shipyard, near the waters edge called 'The Rose & Crown'. Some Friday or Saturday evenings, while Pat was in Aldershot, I used to help the publican, Dot, in 'The Black Buoy' Pub. I think it was there that I learned to play darts quite well.

Before Dot had that Pub, she and her late husband used to own the one near the railway. Growing up I used to play with her son, Derek, during school holidays, mostly on the railway tracks and round about the station. While living at the café I used to go to work on the train - Wivenhoe to The Hythe - while working at the timber merchants along Hawkins Road.

Pat was demobbed out of the army while we were living at the café. So I had lived most of the time without him at his parent's house, then with Aunt Elsie and Uncle George until he finished his two year National Service. We continued to live at the café until we could save enough money for a deposit to buy our own house. Pat was able to go back to work with the firm he had been apprenticed to before going into the Army, so that was very fortunate. Also I was able to continue to work as an invoice, typist and secretary at the builders merchants that I have already mentioned.

Elsie's first Cafe, Wivenhoe

Chapter Eight

"Gayhurst"

Aunt Elsie, who I said had helped me to understand about savings and money, encouraged us to buy our first house. We were about one of the youngest couples in England at that time to buy a house; it was named "Gayhurst" in Belle Vue Road, Wivenhoe, Essex. Belle Vue Road was the 'elite' road in Wivenhoe at that time, which housed mostly retired business people. For instance, the Commodore of the Yacht Club happened to live opposite us in a quite a big house, plus various other well off people along the road. Also, further along was the Wivenhoe Cemetery, where quite a lot of our family graves are. At the entrance from the main road was a hotel, then coming further along was a small sweet shop in the front room of a house. Then a lane way going down towards the village with alms houses on the right hand side, they would have had two rooms downstairs and two upstairs with a small paved back and front yard.

"Gayhurst" was very special to us because it was our first real home that we owned and renovated. We decorated each room with wallpaper, also repainted all the paintwork throughout the house. In some places the wallpaper was almost an inch thick, as the previous occupants over the years had wallpapered layer over layer each time. Friends helped us to soak the walls with water then strip off the old wallpaper with scrappers and knives until the walls were bare, ready to redecorate. Eventually, everyone said that we had made a good job of it. It took quite a long time to tackle each room while we were actually living there. While stripping off the wallpaper I often felt quite nauseated with the smell of the wetness of it not realizing at the time that I was pregnant.

So our first child, a girl whom we named Josephine, was born on 19th October 1960. I was nearly twenty-four years old. Josephine was born in Colchester Maternity Hospital. Husbands were not allowed to be with you then, while the baby was being born. So her father, Pat, went to work and had to wait until visiting time to see the baby. Nanna Tainton came down to stay with us just before and after the birth, to help, as I was quite ill at the time. She really was a good Nanna and loved helping with the baby.

Well a bit about the house. It consisted of a front room, lounge room with steps down to kitchen and laundry area. Upstairs were two double bedrooms and a single bedroom. We made the single bedroom into an ensuite (bathroom and toilet). Pat, being a plumber was able to do the conversion; this was good for us as it was attached to our bedroom. Not many people had an upstairs bathroom, so we felt quite privileged. In the kitchen, there was a Rayburn cooker that was heated by coal or anthracite. You could cook on the hot plates or in the oven, plus in the winter, it warmed the room up very well. It seems a long time ago now, when I think back, to have the coal man come with coal, coke or anthracite for the wood stove. He used to carry these large bags off of the lorry on his back then tip them into our coal shed. The children used to hide sometimes in the coal shed or play in there even though they knew they were not supposed to.

We had a really long narrow garden, with a couple of lawns and sheds. The house had belonged to a nurseryman before we took it over; it had large garden beds planted with Tulips, Iris ('Flags' they were commonly called) and Daffodils, absolutely beautiful. We used to sell the flowers at the front of the house to passers by if they needed any for the cemetery further along the road. Also, we used to supply cut flowers to the greengrocers at the bottom of the village about once a week when in season. The garden doubled out about a third of the way down. Pat dug out a swimming pool at the bottom all by hand but it was never finished. My Cousin, Sylvia, and her fiancé from Coventry came to stay for a holiday with us, when they walked down the back in the evening her fiancé lost his footing and fell into the big swimming pool hole managing to injure himself!

Josephine started school at Wivenhoe Primary School down the village. I used to walk with her along Belle Vue Road, around the corner then down the hill to the school.

A bit later, some of us mothers along our road decided to take turns to take and fetch the children until they were old enough to walk without us. Even then, one of us would wait at the top of the road for them as it was quite busy with traffic. One day waiting they did not come, so after a couple of phone calls, three of us mothers went to look for them. There had been quite a scare with some odd man taking a child over the playing field in the park, which was just up the road across from the school into the cricket shed. Yes, I was right, our daughter Josephine, had decided go and look for herself to see if the man was still there and she took all the other children with her. We found them all playing on the swings in the park, which was out of bounds unless we were with them. They were quite adamant that there was no man in the cricket shed and that we had been making the story up to frighten them not to cross the road after school to go there. Little did they realize what danger they could have been in because the story was true. So they, about six of them, were all in trouble from us mums.

We lived in "Gayhurst" for about eight years. Then we were able to sell the house, retaining the lower half of the property, which was later sold to developers to build houses on. Yes, Pat and I made several friends there and loved living in Wivenhoe, where quite a lot of our relatives lived and are still there today.

The Wivenhoe Cemetery is where we buried my father in 1970; he was only fifty-two years old when he died (his date of birth was 24th June 1918). My sister, Jill, helped me arrange the funeral. Mum didn't come to the funeral as she had left Dad about two years before he died. He died of cancer in the lungs.

Mum died in 2008 at the age of 88 years. She was cremated and her ashes are in the cemetery in Colchester, not with Dad in Wivenhoe. My mother lived with Mick, the chap that she had left Dad for but she had a very unhappy life with that man because he turned out to be an alcoholic. He died a couple of years after Mum.

In the Wivenhoe Cemetery you will find the graves of my father's parents, Frederick Wyatt and his wife Rosina Wyatt. Also Dad's older brothers Frank, Cyril and Jack and his brother in-law Jack Dodson (who was Auntie Winnie's husband) together with other members of the large Wyatt family. Dad's sister, Auntie Lily, plus her husband, Uncle Claude Percival, are also buried there. My very special friends, who died, are also in Wivenhoe Cemetery. Thelma Endean died in 1997 at Christmas time on Boxing night. Then her husband, Terry Endean, died on 2nd April, 2000. They were Godparents to our children Josephine and Ruth. They both had worked very hard for the village of Wivenhoe. At one time, Terry being the Mayor of Wivenhoe, was invited with his wife, Thelma, to the Queen's garden party at Buckingham Palace in London. That was a great honour, not just for them, but also for the whole village, some of whom came to wave them off for the day, including myself.

It used to be strange walking around the cemetery looking out for all the family names. On my mothers' side are: - Nanna Jessie Davey and her husband, my great grandmother and great grandfather (Nanna Tainton's parents), Uncle George, (Nanna Tainton's brother) is buried there, he died 20th June, 1974 aged 66. Then his wife, Elsie, died aged 82 in 1991 and is buried there with him. Nanna Tainton had two other brothers, Uncle Mick Davey and Uncle Bill Davey are also buried there.

While living at "Gayhurst", when Josephine was a baby, I used to walk down to the village pushing her in our 'English style' black high pram. Nearly always I would polish and shine the pram before we went out, then dress her beautifully, she was so precious. Mostly, I would be saying 'Hello' to family members and friends as we walked proudly there and back to do the shopping. Auntie Winnie, who lived on the main street was often out the front in her garden talking to neighbours, so that was another one to talk to. Shopping would often take up most of the morning to get there and back. If we needed to go to the butchers I would go in and have a cup of tea with my friend, Thelma, as their house was adjoined at the back of the butchers shop. When Josephine was old enough to sit up Terry (Thelma's husband the butcher) would sit her on the front counter and make a great fuss over her. Having no children themselves, they thought the world of Josephine and used to love having her to look after for the day if I had to go for an appointment in Colchester or for any other reason.

While walking with a new friend, Joan Clarke, one day to go shopping, she said it seemed that half the village were my relations! Joan and I kept in touch until she went to be with The Lord in 2007. Then her husband, David, died just two years after in 2009. Their daughter, Caroline, got in touch with me by Joan's e-mail address after she had died. It is a blessing being able to use some of the latest technology, even as we are getting older. Joan was a fair bit older than myself, but we were very close friends and kept in touch by mail, phone and of course the e-mail. So it was very thoughtful of Caroline, even though she was very distraught at the time to let me know what had happened. It's lovely to think that Joan's daughter, Caroline, (who still lives in England with her husband and family) are still friends with our Josephine who lives here with her husband and family in Western Australia. They were able to meet up again after many years when Josephine, her husband, Rob, and two children went back to London for a visit.

Back to Wivenhoe. Joan, who lived further along our road, and I used to take it in turns to look after each other's children sometimes during the day. A few years later we became friends with another family who moved in along the road who had six children. Joan then had four, Eileen one, myself two. We were starting to find it difficult to have all these children in one house during our babysitting sessions, so decided to start the first play group in the village, in an old church hall. Of course, it was highly frowned upon but proved to be a great success. In the early 1960's it was considered a terrible sin to leave your babies or young children in the care of other people, even for a short time so that you could go shopping, visiting or keep appointments. We had to get approval from all sorts of places to start the group. Having made a roster of the names of parents and children who had registered with us, mothers could then take turns to stay and help with the group of babies and young children. That freed up some of the other parents to have the morning especially for themselves, giving them a well earned break for a few hours. I remember they dropped them off about 9 am and picked them up at 12 pm midday.

When Josephine was about two and half years old, Caroline about three and a half (that was Joan's eldest child also Michael two years), Joan and I became the foundering members of the Mothers Union in Wivenhoe in 1963. The rector's wife who lived a few doors up the road from us at the Rectory, suggested starting M.U. with our help, also including a few other ladies from our church. The rector and his wife at that time had a daughter, Mary, about the same age as our Josephine. So in 1963, Joan and I were both pregnant, me with Ruth and Joan with Rachael. Ruth and Rachael went to school together in the village and became good friends, both being born in 1964.

As there were quite a few young Mums' that joined our Mothers Union Group, the rectors wife suggested that we branch out and start the M.U. Wivenhoe Young Wives Group. Joan was president and I was secretary for a number of years. We had meetings once a month in the Council Hall having about sixty ladies present. We had excellent speakers, outings, Christmas parties, children's parties and church involvement, which I was happy to help organize with phone calls interviews and paperwork.

One Christmas time we organized a Young Wives children's party for one hundred children from the village. It was quite a big thing for us to do; my job was to see to the catering, which I was happy to do as I have always loved cooking. So Joan and I did most of that between us, making one hundred small jellies, also recruiting other members to help with all that goes with children's parties. It was quite a daunting thing to do, especially at Christmas time involving so many young children.

Mothers Union is the largest World Wide Christian Organization Women's Group in the World, with Head Office at Mary Sumner House in

London. It was named after the founder, Mary Sumner, who started the Mothers Union in 1876. Mary Sumner had her own personal prayer, which I like to pray sometimes. I will put it here for you to read.

Mary Sumner Prayer
All this day, O Lord
Let me touch as many lives as possible for you
And every life I touch, may your Spirit quicken
Whether through the word I speak
The prayer I breathe or the life I live. Amen.

Now that I am living in Australia, I am still a member and was President of M.U. Australia (Mothers Union in Carnarvon branch) Western Australia for 18 years; also I had a turn at being treasurer. At the moment, I have been Vice President for a few years this being 2013. Therefore, I have been a member since I joined in England all those years ago in 1963.

Another thing that Joan and I did was 'Meals on Wheels', when it was our turn on the roster. We used to enjoy this so we called it our day out. After dropping our school age children off at school, we would drive to Wivenhoe University where they prepared the meals. The meals were already hot when we picked them up, they were in metal containers with lids on, inside a larger container that we carried between us to put into the back of the car, then off we would go. We delivered the meals around the village to those who were entitled to them. After letting ourselves in (if they were not able to open the door), we would serve the meals up onto their plates and set them on the table for them. If the person was not able to get to the table, we would put the plates of dinner on a tray on the person's lap. Even though some were very lonely we were not allowed to stay and talk, but could arrange to visit later it necessary.

We used to finish our deliveries about lunchtime, then we would go back to one of our own homes. Our little ones, Ruth and Rachael, helped to clean out the tins before we washed them. Then after our lunch, we took the containers back to the University to be sterilized. We made sure that we could get back home in time for our other children when they came out of school. Joan and I always thought it best for someone to be home for the children after school, so that they did not come home to an empty house.

In England, when children were growing up and attending primary school, we were happy that they did not have homework. Therefore, after school they could have something to eat, get changed out of their uniform (assuming they were wearing one) then could go out to play with their friends. Also, we did not have computers or mobile phones.

While Ruth was a toddler I started having driving lessons. This meant that our next door neighbour, Miss Currie, (a retired headmistress) or my friend, Joan, looked after Ruth while I caught the bus into Colchester, our nearest town. One day however, I had an accident while learning to drive in the British School of Motoring car. I had stopped our vehicle at a junction in the road before turning on to a busy roadway, when a car came down the hill from behind, then crashed into the back of us. My Instructor hurt his leg from the impact of the crash; I had a whiplash on my neck, causing me to have six weeks of heat treatment on the back of the neck. Apparently, the man who drove into the back of us was driving his new car looking at the beautiful sky! He said that he did not realize we had stopped. The impact was quite bad, as it had moved the engine forward in the car we were driving in.

Jessie, Josephine and Ruth

Well, I was able to complete my driving lessons, then surprise, surprise I passed my driving test first time. Friends had tried not encouraging me, as hardly anyone passed first time; they used to call me a 'scatterbrain', so did not think I should even think about driving a car. Pat did try to teach me to drive but that came to a sad end the day that he asked me to do a three point turn on the deserted airport in our good car. What happened was that I backed up and went over the edge of the runway. Let's face it, runways are quite big, so Pat, not having a great sense of humour, did not see the funny side of it. As he shouted at me to get out of the car I just could not stop laughing, so that was the end of his teaching session. That's how come I went to the British School of Motoring in Colchester.

It was so good then not to have to go to town on the bus or train, with baby, bags and pushchair (baby pusher they call them here) as I used to get in such a pickle. But, with the car, I could just load everything in then go in my own time, not having to wait for public transport times.

My sisters, Jean and Jill, were both married before Pat and I, although younger than us, they already had a baby each. Jean with a daughter named Julie and Jill with a son named Peter. When Josephine was born my sister Jeans' daughter, Julie, was already three years old. In the same year that Julie was born, my mother gave birth to my youngest sister, Jasmine. Therefore, Jasmine was an auntie as soon as she came into the world. It seemed odd that mother and daughter had a baby in the same year. They were born while I was still living at home that was at 60 Barn Hall Avenue; that was before Pat and I were married.

From the time Jasmine was born I helped to look after her, especially while she was a baby until she was around two years old, when I moved out to get married. Jasmine was my parents seventh child. I was still helping to look after the others which were boys, Christopher, Cyril and Clive, mostly by cooking and helping with the washing. We did have a washing machine, especially for the sheets and large items in the laundry room and a large trough, which we soaked the clothes in and washed a lot by hand. Jill also was a good helper, as on Saturday mornings we took turns with the washing. The long linen lines stretched the whole length of the garden and were filled with lovely clean sheets. My sister, Jean, had left home, and was busy in her flat in town looking after her baby daughter, Julie.

I had decided that I would like a large family myself, so when Josephine came along it was great, she

Josephine and Ruth in 1968

was so beautiful to me because I had longed so much for my own little family, then our second beautiful daughter, Ruth came along in 1964. She too, was born in the Colchester Maternity Hospital. My special friends, Thelma and Terry, looked after Josephine while I was giving birth to Ruth. They asked to have Josephine to keep as their own child, thinking that I would not be well enough to look after two children. Although, I loved my friends dearly, I just couldn't let them have her to keep. We shared a very close relationship and they both loved all of our children. It was so sad that they were not able to have children themselves. We were delighted that they accepted to be Godparents for Josephine and Ruth.

Pat and I became self employed the week Josephine was born. Pat, being a plumber and heating engineer, went into partnership with another chap, Peter Beddoes. I did the secretarial work, using our home, which needless to say often resembled an office. I was very fortunate being able to afford to have someone come in to do the housework once a week, as I was finding it difficult using the vacuum cleaner because it pulled on my chest, which was still quite painful at times. Some people used to say that I should never have children, not realizing that even when a person is ill with any disease, they still long to have a normal life and all that goes with it.

Josephine, Ruth and Jessie

Chapter Nine

Brightlingsea

We moved house from "Gayhurst", Belle Vue Road in Wivenhoe Essex to 5 Stanley Road, Brightlingsea, in Essex, U.K. It was on the corner of George Avenue. That was a small seaside town. We moved there before Matthew was born. There was only the one road to get into Brightlingsea and out again. I remember driving up the small steep hill going into Brightlingsea and back down hill out of the village. Colchester was our nearest large town. What makes me remember this is the snow, because in the winter months that road was very treacherous, because of the black ice under the snow, being quite narrow and just a small two-way traffic road, it could be quite frightening going up or down it.

While living there in 1968, our son, Matthew, was born. During all those years, I still had lots of problems with my health, mainly my chest plus ear problems and catarrh, very bad hay fever and asthma, that had started when I was in my early 20's.

I didn't go to the doctors regarding my last pregnancy until I was three months pregnant. The doctor was quite emphatic that I should not go ahead with the pregnancy and asked me to consider having the baby terminated. In those days they only terminated them if the patients' life was at risk and he was shocked that I had conceived again, knowing the state of my health. After having X-rays for my chest to see what state it was in for the pregnancy (as I did not want an abortion), the results showed that the bronchiectasis had come back and, this time, it had also spread to what had been my good lung. I was determined not to have the baby killed because I believed that God would look after us, also I agreed to have my tubes tied after the birth.

The doctor tried to tell me how serious the illness was and how worse it would get if I carried on with the pregnancy but, I asked God if I could keep the baby and dedicated it to Him. Those of us who know that babies are a gift from God shudder at the thought of abortion, because we know that life begins at or even before the moment of conception and every life is precious to God who made us.

For most of the nine months I had to rest as much as I could, which was difficult with a young family. I had thrombosis in my legs and had difficulty walking sometimes; it was good being able to drive, but difficult to walk around town shopping. My sister, Jill, often came with me; meeting me in town and waiting for me to sit down, wherever we found a seat or a chair in some of the shops. As for my other sisters it wasn't possible for my young sister, Jasmine, to come as she was still at school and Jean had remarried and was living in America.

When the baby contractions started, I was taken into the Colchester Maternity Hospital. After being in labour for the day the baby decided not to appear. So next day I was taken home and we had another try a week later. Our son, Matthew, was born 16th September 1968. It was a difficult birth and I could not have gas because of the state of my lungs, so they gave me something else to help my breathing. When, halfway through the delivery, the medication seemed to cause the baby to go to sleep, I was fortunate enough to watch our son being born and was able to hold him to see that, yes, he was a boy baby. Then I was taken back to the ward to rest.

Later, when they bought the babies around for us mothers to feed (they were all snugly wrapped up) I said they had bought the wrong one. It caused quite a problem, they insisted that I could not possibly know because they looked different when they were washed and wrapped snugly in their blankets. This was a lot of nonsense because I had seen the face of my baby and was positive I knew the difference. Well, Larman was not a common name and for about the first time there was another Larman in the nursing home. Matron, who seemed most formidable, was informed and came in with the two Larman babies and asked me to point out which I thought was mine. Then she promptly laid the one I had said was my baby boy on the bed. She said I was to undo its nappy to see if I had chosen right, which I had, as apparently the other when uncovered was a girl baby. (Matron by the way had not been told which sex any of the babies were at that time. She had just been called in to access the situation).

Praise The Lord I chose the right baby and was asked if I wanted to take the matter further because of the incompetence that had gone on. As I was so thankful to have the right one I said no, it was just as well that the other mother knew nothing of this.

My health was very bad at this time. While I was looking after the baby one day in the hospital nursery, blood just suddenly poured from me and I was put back in bed with tablets to thicken my blood, whereas before I had been having tablets to thin the blood to stop it clotting i.e. thrombosis. Also I still had to measure my legs most days, trying to keep off of them when they were not feeling too good. I know for sure now that whatever medication one is on, that it can go through into the womb and affect the baby. We had a dreadful time when we got our new baby boy home.

For about three years we had no proper sleep, as he was hyperactive, suffered from fits, then was diagnosed asthmatic at about eighteen months. I praise The Lord that he is perfectly normal now. Before being born into this world, while he was still in the womb, sometimes he would rock from side to side, you could see the fast movement just by watching my stomach. One day I was sitting outside in our back garden reading, near the side wall, saying 'Hello' to neighbours walking past, when one stood and watched quite fascinated to see my tummy moving fast from side to side. This would go on for five minutes or more and was quite exhausting.

My health really did deteriorate, I was ill not only during the winter months now but most of the summer when the hay fever season started, then I needed to inhale from a face mask before getting out of bed some mornings. With three young children, it was usually a challenge to get them ready – Josephine for school and Ruth to a private nursery school plus the new baby to be fed and watered. Pat had to leave early for his plumbing work so could not help at that time of day.

Well, 5 Stanley Avenue was a big old house on a corner with a very small front garden plus a small paved back yard incorporating a garage. It had a beautiful small front porch; the door had lovely stain glass windows, plus stain glass side windows. There were big old hospital type radiators throughout the house. Inside was a hallway, so by the front door we had corner shelves and were able to have a phone on one of these. The hallway and stairs we covered with dark red raised type of carpet and white painted stair rails. It looked lovely.

No 5 Stanley Avenue, Brightlingsea

The staircase wound up to the bedroom area where there were four bedrooms and a large bathroom. We thought that we had made a beautiful job of the bathroom giving the very high ceiling a coat of navy blue paint and the floor covered with navy blue carpet. We made a step the length of the bath and covered it with carpet so that it was easier to get in an out of, also for me to kneel and bath the children. Downstairs they were really good large rooms with very high ceilings. So from the front door there was a hallway with the front room on the right hand side, then along to the dining room, which also had stain glass windows in the door. Then turn right into the kitchen/come breakfast/room straight through to the laundry with large walk in pantry.

We renovated the whole house, making a breakfast bar in the large kitchen (that would have been a very modern thing to do then). In the sink area we put a deep sink incorporating a top loading dish washer, which doubled as a washing machine as the agitator was in the bottom of the sink. This I thought was very cleaver and constantly in use for one or the other applications, plus it had a normal sink included next to it. The old walk-in pantry to me was a blessing, as it had a very large marble shelf, which kept things beautifully cool. It was one of the nicest houses, when we had finished taking out all the old hospital radiators and replacing them with modern slimline ones.

Being pregnant with Matthew while we lived there I also started my painting career, going to night school at the Brightlingsea High School. A lady friend in the village asked me to go with her for company but I found it very hard to leave our Ruth as she used to get very distressed if I was not there for her.

However, this lady persuaded me to go, saying that I should have an interest other than staying at home most of the time. She pointed out that Pat had a night out each week with his friend, Michael, to go to the Pub and that I should have a night out each week if I would like to. Well, I was glad that I made the effort as I made friends with the art teacher, Leon and his wife Margaret. Margaret was also pregnant at the time as myself with her daughter, Clare, who was born about the same time as our son Matthew in September 1968. So, I have been painting since then, being very fortunate to have exhibitions over the years, to sell some of my paintings, also to teach, which I am still doing.

Josephine went to Brightlingsea High School where Leon's wife was a teacher. Margaret was a beautiful piano player and used to love to sing Opera. Sometimes in the summer months after school we would go straight to the beach for a while, calling in at the Co-op for some sweets or crisps to take with us. There was a salt-water pool at the beach for the children to paddle or swim in with a walkway around to cut it off from the sea. The water used to come over the concrete walkway when the tide came in so the water was always fresh, washing up onto the beach, where we used to sit with friends after school and watch the children play in the water or paddle and swim with them. While sitting with Matthew (a baby then) talking to another young mother, I looked up to see our Ruth struggling in the water. I rushed in with my clothes on and grabbed her by the hair as she was going under again and carried her back to the beach. It is amazing when you think of it; other parents were standing around knee deep in water right next to her and never heard her cries for help. They probably thought she was playing about. We were very fortunate not to have lost her.

Ruth went to a private Nursery School because she was not happy with a lot of children running around in the playgroup situation, she was very shy, finding it difficult to talk and communicate with people until she was about four years old.

While living at Brightlingsea, Josephine was used as a photographer's model, which was very nice. The beautiful portrait photo's were displayed in an exhibition in the Colchester Castle. We still have one of the lovely large photo's plus some smaller ones.

The girls went to Roman Catholic Sunday school lessons, which were held one afternoon a week after school at the priest's house. So I sometimes took them to the Anglican Church with me, which was on the way in/out of Brightlingsea at the top of the hill going into the town.

While living at 5 Stanley Avenue, for the first time, I organized an art exhibition for my own artwork and that of the surrounding villages. It was a great success with lots of paintings and people. We raised quite a lot of money for a charity. Well, we renovated our house. It was beautiful when we had finished it. But we needed to move again after only being there a couple of years.

So we moved out of Brightlingsea to Alresford, (Alresford is between Brightlingsea and Wivenhoe). I packed the car overnight ready to take off early next morning, then during the night we had more snow, it was so deep that we couldn't get the car out. We would have got through that road going out of Brightlingsea only with chains on the tyres and we didn't have those. Chains were one of those things we thought we might get and never did. The car I had at that time was an M.G. with a twin exhaust; it was bottle green, a lovely little car. Pat had a van for his plumbing work that seemed to drive better in the snow than my car. So it took us a few days going back and forth taking personal things before the removal van came to take the furniture and packing boxes.

Chapter Ten

Alresford

Alresford is a small village, not far from where we lived at "Gayhurst", in Wivenhoe. It was there at Alresford, we decided to emigrate to Australia, which we did in 1973. So, you wonder how we decided to emigrate. Well, we did try years before when Josephine was small, but our papers seemed to have disappeared or got lost somehow, so Pat put an end to us leaving the U.K.

Later about 1970, I had become so ill that my chances of surviving were down to a couple of years, unless I could escape the English winters. The reason we decided to emigrate to a warmer climate were really for health problems. However, it was not that easy as I had to prove that I would not be a burden on the state once we were here. Medically, they would not pass me to go, so we tried private medicals, which took quite a while in regard to tests. Also I had to agree that I would not claim for a medical pension in Australia. So after a lot of paper work and specialist reports we were finally accepted. Then we had to transfer funds before we left and Pat had to agree to look for work once we were here. We had a Sponsor which also helped us to be accepted for emigration.

Anyway back to Alresford where we bought "The Laurels". When we bought "The Laurels" in Alresford, it was also in need of renovation. So starting on the kitchen area, we then built on to the back of the house. We built a laundry room, a large playroom plus a studio that doubled as an office. The studio was quite large with French windows on the two opposite walls including sidelights, both opening up into the garden. That meant those two walls were nearly all glass to let the light in for my paintings.

This house had a lovely long garden that backed onto the railway line. We soon got

"The Laurels", Alresford, UK 1973

used to hearing the trains go past, so they were not a problem to us. Between the house and the railway there were fruit trees with a pathway through the middle of them. Beautiful apples, plums, greengages and green apples, which we used to store in boxes in an upstairs room for the winter months. There were lovely Bramley and Cox's orange pippin apples being amongst them.

In the kitchen we put an illuminated ceiling, it was something special. I remember my cousin, Sylvia, and her husband, Frank, looking for ages to find the light switch to turn them off, not realizing that it was just behind the fridge. They had come down from Coventry to stay for a holiday with us. We had gone upstairs to bed the first night they were there, leaving them to turn off the lights, as they were sleeping on the bed settee in the lounge room area. The whole of the kitchen ceiling was illuminated; those two rooms were open plan living so it was too bright for them to sleep. However, eventually they were thankful to locate the switch after feeling around the walls in both rooms.

Different radiators we installed throughout the house to show clients what they looked like when they were choosing their particular central heating. Mostly we had the slimline and slimline double radiators put under the windows in the lounge room and front room. We turned them on their sides at the bottom of the stairs and in the kitchen where we had pulled part of the wall down to have open style living, incorporating the lounge room and kitchen with breakfast area as well which doubled as dining room. Skirting heating we put all around the rooms in the studio and playroom. This was oil fired heating with the boiler room outside, which was controlled from inside the house in the kitchen. We could set the heating to come on before we got up to warm the house and set it to turn off, when we had been in bed for a while. Yes, we had radiators in all the four bedrooms, bathroom and landing.

Thinking of the bedrooms in this house, reminds me that we had to partition the girls bedroom with a divider down the middle so that they could have their own space. The reason was that they did not agree with each other as they were growing up. Well, like most children were not keen to tidy their rooms and at one time Josephine's side was such a mess of children's toys and papers that it was not right to let the cleaning lady go in. So when she came home on the school bus that day, as she walked across the front lawn, I opened the bedroom window and threw down the papers to blow in the wind across the lawn to her feet. It was a big learning curve to hopefully teach her to be a bit tidier. Whereupon she told me it was the cleaning lady's job. Well, there we are, we all have to learn to live together and sometimes it is not that easy. She still remembers looking up and seeing things being thrown out of the upstairs window.

Why we built on the large playroom, was because in the winter time, it is sometimes too cold for the children go out to play. This was a welcome addition to our home because we used to have several children come to visit and play. We bought an old cheap piano and put it in the playroom for the children to practice on. Later, we gave this piano to my brother, Christopher, when we moved. He painted it white, put it in the front room of his council house and used to love playing by ear. It made a change from him playing the drums. Once he persuaded me to paint a picture on the drum skin, before playing in a pantomime.

Josephine had piano lessons with the teacher coming to the house once a week. Our good piano was kept in the front room. In England the front room was always kept for special occasions, so was not used that often. Suddenly, after a lesson one week she decided to cancel the lessons, not only was the teacher surprised but so were we, as she had made no mention of the fact that she did not want to continue. That was a shame, as she was doing very well. However, it is no good trying to make children do something if their heart is not in it, unless of course it is really necessary for their education.

The studio doubled up as an office, where we used to do the paper work and phone calls for our plumbing and heating business. Pat, and his business partner, Peter Beddoes, were kept very busy with plenty of work; they were excellent plumbers and well sought after, attracting much work on new houses and housing estates.

Yes, I did oil paintings in the studio. Sometimes during the summer months, I used to take my paints and easel out into the back garden to paint, while Matthew could play or go in the little blow up paddling pool. Our neighbour who bought several of my paintings looked over the fence one day and took a liking to a large landscape that I was working on; she swapped me for a small caravan when it was finished. Mostly, I was painting in "oils" and was involved with art exhibitions.

During my pottery sessions, I remember making a fountain that Pat plumbed into the gold fishpond he had made, which was situated outside the studio windows in the back garden. He organized it so that the water would come up and recycle through the top of the fountain. He plugged it into the electricity somehow so that it could be turned on and off from inside the house. It wasn't very big but we thought it was great.

Matthew was still a very sick little boy while we lived at "The Laurels". He was diagnosed with asthma and also had fits, which we had medication for. Our cleaning lady, at that time, left because she couldn't cope with helping me to administer his medication and seeing him as he was. Praise The Lord that he grew out of all those things when we came to Australia.

My father died of cancer of the lungs while we were living in that house; he was only fifty-two years old. Dad stayed with us for a few days after coming out of hospital, then he went back home to 60 Barn Hall Avenue, where he lived just across the road from Jill. He used to walk across to her house most mornings for a cup of tea. Then one morning she phoned to say that Dad had collapsed onto the floor and she could not help him up. So we phoned the doctor, who organized for him to go to hospital. I called into Auntie Lily's house (Dad's sister) at Alresford on my way through to Wivenhoe, then on to Colchester Hospital. Auntie Lily got in touch with the rest of Dad's side of the family as we were told that it would most likely be his last day.

Nanna Tainton came with Jill and me to the hospital to see Dad, her son-in-law, for the last time. Nanna was a great comfort to us all. Christopher, Cyril (with his girlfriend Kate), Clive and Jasmine, (who was still at school), were still living at home when Dad died, so we had to get permission for them to stay in the house. The boys were all working, so, although they were under age to rent the property, the Council agreed to let them continue with the rent and live there. It did help that Jill lived just across the road to make sure things would work out alright.

As my mother had previously left Dad two years before he died, it was left to me to organize the funeral. When I asked Nanna Tainton about it, she said that as the eldest of Dad's children I must learn to do these things. She was very helpful advising us. So my sister, Jill, came with me to help arrange everything; she was a real blessing. Everything went off as planned with our family and the aunts coming to Wivenhoe Cemetery, where most of the old family graves are.

Josephine started going to Girl Guides at Alresford which I believe is still an excellent organization. She was attending Brightlingsea High School at this time, having to go on the school bus there and back each day while Ruth attended the local Alresford Primary School. At School

Ruth made friends with a young girl her age, also named Ruth. Ruth's friend's family immigrated to Australia before us and they gave us their address just in case we would be able to meet up with them when we emigrated. It was very fortunate that our Ruth's friend's father, Geoff, who was a carpenter, knew Pat through work commitments in England. Some other friends who lived in Alresford, had previously been to Australia, and then came back to England only to decide to go back again. Josephine had made friends with Philip, one of their son's, so both girls knew someone to look out for when we emigrated here.

On Sundays Josephine and Ruth came to the Anglican Church in Alresford for Sunday School as there was no Roman Catholic Church there. We had a lot of taking and fetching to do in regard to the children, for school and after school activities. Living out of town, it was best to have our own transport. I was fortunate enough to have a new Citroen-Ami 8 car to drive, so I was very sad having to leave it behind when we emigrated.

Our house which had been on the market for sometime had still not sold, when it was time for us to leave. So we left it in the hands of the real estate agent, with our next door neighbours also kindly keeping an eye on the property. It was sad to leave all our lovely furniture, plus lots of possessions there. The children could only bring one or two things with them and had to leave most of their precious play things behind. Of course, they were not too happy about that but were looking forward to having new bikes and other toys in Australia.

My friend, Thelma, helped me to pack a large trunk and some cases with household things. We wrapped them in clothes instead of the newspaper that people often used. Both of us were very tearful, thinking that we may not be seeing each other again. Terry came and he cried as well, asking us not to go. But when you think it is right to go, then you have to go. Then my friend, Joan, came to the house to say goodbye, it was all so sad.

Pat at this stage changed his mind and said he was not leaving England. However, as we only had a family passport (not one each). He decided, yes, he would come and then leave me here with the children and then go back. I am thankful that once we were here in Australia he did stay. There were reasons why he wanted to go back but we won't go into those now.

The saddest thing of all was to leave our family and friends in

England, many of whom came to wave us off at North Station, Colchester, on the train heading for London on the 3rd of January 1973. So as not to get too upset at leaving our family, we decided to pretend we were just going for a holiday. Pat and I had saved enough money for our fare back to England, just supposing we were not happy with the move to Australia.

Once in London, we made our way to Heathrow airport to board the plane for Perth, Western Australia. Heathrow is a very large airport and yes, we had to hunt for one of the children who got lost in the crowds, thankfully we found her before too long. Everyone was getting very tired and anxious after getting up early, because of all the travelling that was needed for us to get from Alresford to Colchester, then on to London's Heathrow airport.

The trip on the plane seemed to be a very long trip, coming over with three children to look after, Josephine 12 years, Ruth 8 years and Matthew 4 years old. The stopover was for a few hours at Singapore, where we were able to look around, stretch our legs after sitting so long in the plane and purchase a souvenir for each of the children. The humidity and heat at Singapore airport was quite foreign to us having just left a very cold winter in England. Also we had never been in tropical heat or humidity before. Then back on to the plane for our destination to Western Australia, which took well over twenty hours flying time from U.K.

Chapter Eleven

Australia.

When we stepped off the plane at Perth airport, it was beautiful and warm with no humidity. It was dark but there was plenty of lighting around the airport. We waited by some palm trees for the agent to pick us up. There was a soft breeze blowing beautiful warm air all around us and I felt a lovely peace that we were here. It just seemed as if I had come home.

It had been difficult getting through the emigration procedures because of my health problems, when we first applied to come here but at last we had been accepted. It was wonderful to know that we had come here to the warmth of this country. I have never really felt much homesickness, except for the large family that we left behind. We have always been a close family, being the eldest of seven children and partly a mother to some of them, it was as if I had left some of my own children behind. However we still keep in touch and some have been out here to visit. As time goes by, some of the others will hopefully be able to come.

Once here we were taken to live in a rented flat at Lynwood, which was a suburb of Perth. Inside the flat it was very hot, being on the first floor with no air conditioners just ceiling fans, which moved the heat around at a fast rate. We spent most of the first night drinking cold water and cordial, trying to keep cool. Just two small bedrooms – so the three children were squashed into bunk beds in one room and Pat and I in the other. It was not possible for us to stay there very long in those conditions.

We decided to purchase a car, a Holden station wagon, which seemed quite large for us to drive but was a very sensible vehicle for us to have. Although we both had our British driving licenses, it was compulsory to take a test for an Australian one, so we did that before becoming the proud owners of our new (second hand) vehicle. The Holden station wagon served us well for many years; however it did not have an air conditioner in it all those years ago. So we had many long journeys travelling up North with wet towels around us and the windows open, which of course let in all the heat. Pat needed the windows open he said for the breeze to come in, well, it was certainly a hot breeze. A lot of our long distance travelling was done late in the day and through the cooler part of the night.

Next then we moved to Brentwood into a rented house, while we looked around for a ready built home. The main reason we left the flat, was because we had been sponsored to come over with a housing firm who said they had new houses for us to choose from and purchase one of their properties on our arrival. However, they did not exist when we arrived so they suggested that we let them build us one. Well, that was not the best idea with three small children to look after in a new country. Also Pat needed to find employment and for us to find schools for Josephine and Ruth as well as a nursery school for Matthew. We did not realize that the signs for 'nursery' in Australia meant for plants and for children the nursery schools are called Day Care Centres. We had a bit of learning to do because apparently what we really needed was pre-primary school and there was a waiting list, so that was the end of that for a while.

It was quite good living at Brentwood, which was not too far from an excellent shopping centre and a beautiful lake. Josephine and Ruth could go to school alright from there and Pat to work as a plumber in Perth. I stayed home to look after Matthew as we could not get him into a preschool. While at Brentwood in the rented house, we started to look around for a house to purchase.

Chapter Twelve

"Greenacres" at Sawyers Valley

Eventually, we found an old derelict orchard in Sawyers Valley, which is up in the hills just past Mundaring near Perth. There we learnt what a caveat was. It was something new to us coming from England. We were actually in the house when the phone rang and someone said that the house belonged to them as well and they wanted their part of the money we had paid for it. So sitting on the floor in the hallway I contacted our solicitor, who said - that there were six people involved, all had caveats on the property. He said we were quite entitled to stay in the house while he sorted it out as some of the people concerned were abroad. How we understood the situation was the fact that the people who were selling the property to us (they were of Greek nationality) had not paid the previous owners or the ones before themselves. This meant three sets of husband's and wife's, including the people who were selling it to us, had to obtain our money then pay the others. Until all were contacted, we would not be able to have the title deeds and sign for them. What a mess. Well, we had paid our deposit, so were allowed to stay until all the caveat people were contacted to sign the agreement that we could buy the property at the price we offered. Praise The Lord that it all worked out in the end.

The price we offered was for them to leave the bedroom furniture in the deal (as we had none) and a few other odd things. We are still using furniture from the orchard house that we bought from them in 1973 and it is still in good condition after our purchase of it approx 40 years ago this year being 2013.

I would like to tell you a bit about the Sawyers Valley property. Firstly, we liked the place, although it had been run down and not lived in properly for about two years. The owners had been driving up at the weekends, picking fruit, collecting the eggs and leaving because they were then running a business and living in Perth. It was a large old weatherboard house with verandas at the front, back and around one side.

We had met up with some people when we first came to Australia whose son Pat knew through work in England. He had given us his parents address asking us to get in contact with them when we arrived here. We became good friends and they gave us a hand to paint the place out. It took us six weekends with big tins of white emulsion to paint through the kitchen and lounge room so that we could move in and renovate the rest of the house while living in it.

It was March, 1973 when we discovered the property and things from the previous Christmas were still unwashed on the tables in the kitchen where they had been celebrating. Food was still in containers in the cupboards and under the sink. All of which had to be thrown out due to mould and bugs. When we started cleaning in the kitchen cupboards, hundreds of large things with wings flew out and crawled up the walls to the high ceilings. My friend and I retreated with a scream to the next room. Her husband explained to us that they were big brown and shiny cockroaches. We had never seen such things, he said they had to be sprayed and killed. The whole house had to be sprayed for cockroaches, spiders and other creepy crawlies before we could live in it.

The time came for us to move in. When the removal men moved us in they asked if we really were going to stay there that night as they said it was more like camping out, except we would be inside. However, we convinced them we would be all right and they shook their heads and left us to it. Our friends invited us to stay with them until we had more furniture and cleaned the place up a bit more. But we declined saying that we would prefer to be there on hand to get thing shipshape.

The house was old, but stable with a tin roof. It was quite a novelty to us because, in England, this would not have been allowed. When the torrential rain came on the tin roof, which was not insulated, it was something to be believed. It thundered down so hard, you could not hear yourself speak; it was quite deafening. I think the rest of the house was made up mostly of timber and weatherboard with good shady verandah's.

The large front room had an open fireplace big enough to put good size logs on for a wood fire. One wall had wood and glass sliding doors leading to a big lounge room which also had an open fireplace for a log fire. These were definitely needed in the winter months up in the hills, as it gets very cold. There were five bedrooms and a decent size kitchen in that house. A patio out the back was covered with grape vines, also grape vines along the front fence line. There were about six or more varieties of grapes including Lady Fingers, Seedless Sultana, Muscat, small wine grapes, large round white grapes in various places. Some were hanging down over our heads on the walkway to the linen line out the back. All had been left to fend for themselves and had the most incredible huge bunches hanging from them, that we had ever seen. One of the oddest things to see would have been one of our greyhounds, 'Skippy', walk up to the Lady Finger grapes that were hanging quite low down along the front fence, pick one off in his mouth, then sit on the grass and eat it.

After sweeping the back patio for a couple of weeks, which was covered with feathers from the chickens plus chicken droppings, we realized that there were paving slabs there. So, Pat and myself got to work with shovels and found we had a good paved back patio under the debris. This patio led from the back door along the back of the house to the outside bathroom and toilet. The shower was very dangerous in the bathroom because to turn on the hot water the electric switch was at the back of the shower where the water came down onto you. It was a very dodgy arrangement. The 'roman' bath which you had to stand in to shower was very good for Matthew and his little girl friend (Katrina) to sit in and play, to keep cool during the long hot summer. Katrina was around the same age as Matthew, about four and a half years old. I had agreed to look after her during weekdays, while her parents worked. There was no place in a playgroup or pre-primary school for them.

Katrina's parents lived at the top end of our orchard so it was easy for them to drop her off or let her come through the fence and run down to the house. The children got on well and were good company for each other while Pat and I worked on the property. I looked after Katrina for a year, while the father, who had obtained a grant, worked at home writing a book and her mother went out to work.

On our property there were plenty of fruit trees. We had Granny Smith apples, mandarins, pears, peaches, plums and oranges. In all there were eighteen acres, with a fifty-foot dam on the property that had about thirty to forty ducks on it. An old historic pioneer cottage on the property, was used as a shed with hundreds of pigeons living in the roof space. The pigeons used to fly, circling over Sawyers Valley each day. Our neighbours were not amused when they started eating their new seedlings. So, they came one night with sacks, filled them with some of those pigeons to take them away. The neighbours had waited until it was dark then went into the cottage with torches to collect quite a lot of them. Also, regarding the ducks, one neighbour shot some to eat, as he said they were walking through and flying over his fence eating his crops.

We found we had a pigsty, so we renewed the pig license and bought three piglets. The pigs were to share between our neighbours further along the road and us. The neighbour's wife brought two buckets of goat's milk every few days to feed the pigs that she had left over from feeding her family of six children. One large beautiful goat my neighbour had, would be taken into the kitchen to milk. Some mornings I would go around for a cuppa after dropping our children Ruth and Matthew off at the Mount Helena Primary School. The large light brown coloured goat would be standing there, nibbling a slice of bread from the kitchen table, while she was being milked into a bucket on the kitchen floor.

We used to let the pigs out into the orchard to scavenge and eat the dropped apples. They grew into beautiful great big pigs. Then the time came to eat them…so we had to get another neighbour to kill them for us. The first pig was divided between those friends who brought the goat milk and ourselves. Well, we cut it up then put it into our respective freezers. While it was cooking it smelt just like pork with apple sauce (they had eaten so many apples). It truly was the nicest pork. The lady who was in partnership with us regarding the pigs, cried over the phone because she felt she was eating a friend, especially after bringing milk from their goat and getting to know the pigs. It was difficult to console her regarding this, so the best way was to say - think of it as meat when you take it out of the freezer, just like you would buy at the butchers shop. Well of course they did eventually eat it and thought it was excellent.

With another pig, we decided to cook it on a spit out the back of the house. That was the time we were going to have a B.B.Q. to celebrate with our friends. There were about sixty or more people coming to the B.B.Q on that Saturday evening. Pat got the pig set up ready to be cooked on the spit in a big clear area out the back, then he left about 5 am. He was on duty for the fire brigade, so he left instructions for me to light the fire under it at 7 am. At 9 am one of our friends from the City in Perth rang to say that there was a fire ban and that spotter planes were out. We thought that she was joking, however she said it had been on the news and for us to listen to the next news. After hearing about the spotter planes on the radio, we then had to put the fire out. Have you ever tried putting out a campfire with out making any smoke? We had more smoke from it putting it out than trying to light it!

Anyway we did it, then what to do with the pig because it was still uncooked. Pat's parents were out from England, staying with us for a holiday at that time. So they helped me to bring the pig in and put it onto the kitchen table. It was still attached to the stake that went through the length of it when it was on the spit; it was very large and heavy. Pat was still out with the fire brigade while this was going on.

Well, we cut it up into pieces; joints etc., then spent all day cooking it. Some of the pork we cooked in the very small old ancient oven that I had, some on top of the stove in frying pans, under the grill and in our electric frypan. There is a lot of meat on a large pig! However a couple of huge leg joints we put in the freezer for another time.

We couldn't get in touch with the people that were coming to tell them what was happening, so had to carry on with preparing food for the evening celebration, (at the moment I cannot remember what it was in aid of but 60 or more people were a lot to cater for). Never mind eh!

It was that day Matthew's cat decided to have kittens in the wardrobe in his bedroom, giving birth on top of some of his clothes that were lying on the inside at the bottom. Another mess to clear up, which had to be left till the next day due to cooking pig! One of our greyhounds ('Lady') was very pregnant at the time so she was hiding up, trying to find somewhere to give birth. It was a very busy day.

Another thing I remember about the pigs (that is, before we ate them), is - the day that Pat suddenly took off with two of our friend's husband's, whose families were visiting for the day. They went running after the pigs, which were fully grown by then, along the road out the front of the house where they had gone when they escaped from the pig sty. Myself, our friends, plus children stood on the outside garden seats with the pigs running around us when they got them back through the gate. Everyone was terrified of these three great big creatures running around with two large greyhounds in pursuit. Then we saw the funny side and just laughed, looking at each other standing on the wooden seats, three ladies and eight children. The three dad's managed to get them back into the pig sty, then sat and had a well deserved beer.

What else to tell you of the orchard property? Well, it was such a shambles to start with that we called it "Green Acres", because it reminded us of a funny T.V. show that we used to watch. The power used to go off quite frequently. Guess where the meter box was? It was half way up the orchard nailed onto a tree. Nearly every time it poured down with tropical rain, the power would go off. Pat would have to put on gum boots, a raincoat, plus hat, then armed with a torch, (if it was night-time), and pliers would make his way to the meter box. It was wired up with the most extraordinary pieces of wire and metal, none of which seemed to be electrical wire. It was a wonder that any power on the place worked.

While living there in Sawyers Valley we had the most rainfall that had fallen there for over seventeen years. We were very wet and cold in the winter and nearly cooked by the heat of the summer. Very different from the English weather that we had grown up with and were used to.

When we bought the house it still had blackout blinds up at some of the windows, left over from the war years. The blinds came in handy. We left them so that when Matthew, who was four and a half years old, went to bed we could darken his room beautifully, also the blackout blinds helped to keep it cool in the summer. That summer, when Matthew was five years old in September, we bought him a bicycle for his birthday; it was one of the best presents we could have bought him. You see, he was asthmatic at the time so when he learnt to ride his two-wheeler bicycle up and down the orchard, it helped to strengthen his lungs and his breathing. One time when he was just learning he fell off and immediately went into an asthma attack. 'Skippy' our greyhound alerted us by barking and standing beside him in the long grass. After administering his medicine and waiting a while he was then ready to go again.

"Greenacres", Sawyers Valley, Western Australia 1973

Like I said earlier, in each lounge room there were large open fireplaces that we could put big logs on and leave them smouldering overnight to keep the house warm in the winter. So! we had the excitement of a chimney fire! One morning as I was putting newspaper on the almost dead embers to get the fire going, some newspaper was drawn up the chimney alight, then flames and smoke roared out the top, which brought Pat running like crazy down the orchard into the house to sort it out.

That was when Nanna Tainton was staying with us, poor soul; it was a big fright for her to hear the roaring of the fire going up the chimney, and for me too, might I add. Thank goodness Pat was able to help us put it out; also he was pretty cross with me for letting it get out of hand.

Nanna had come out from England to stay for a holiday, then, if she liked it here, she would have lived with us. But it was all too much for her, the wide-open spaces, as was the long distances for travelling. While she was on holiday with us, Nanna, myself and Matthew, caught some dreadful flu virus and had to be looked after in our respective bedrooms by Pat, who had to spoon medicine into us all as we were too sick to even hold the spoon. Although Nanna loved being with us she decided to go back to England to her own little house. The vastness of Australia was a bit too much for her and of course she missed the rest of the family in England.

What else can I tell you? Pat was encouraged to join the Bush Fire Brigade not long after we had moved onto the orchard property. When the chaps brought the fire engine to show us we laughed and laughed, it looked like something out of the 'Key Stone Cops' films. We thought they were playing a joke on us, but we found out that it was for real and the fire truck was kept at the end of our road in a shed. Pat was told he should join, so was given a key to the fire truck shed after they had taken him for a drive around in it and instructed him on how it all worked. That was all there was in those days (that was 1973) to fight the huge bush fires that used to, and still do, ravish the dry countryside each summer.

We were there when there was a very bad bush fire one year. The fire leapt over the Great Eastern Highway, burnt through Sawyers Valley, Stoneville, Mt. Helena and all around that area including part of St. John National Park. At one time Pat was amongst the firemen who just got out with their lives when they were fire fighting. A small fire engine with limited water was no match for those extensive fires in the hills around the City of Perth.

One day while I was driving the children home from school, we suddenly found the tall trees in front of us on fire. I was able to quickly turn the car around and go back the way we had come, then turn up the next road away from the fire to get home a different way. Praise The Lord that we made it alright. We hosed our house down ready for the fire to come on to our property and were very fortunate that it only came on one side of the orchard during the day and we were able to contain it. However, during the night we up fire fighting again as it was burning around our fence line, sadly demolishing most of our lovely grape vines, also the bushes at the front of the property and along one side by the road.

Next day we drove around Stoneville and Mt. Helena, it looked like something from another planet. Everywhere was blackened; grass, plants, also trees were smouldering due to the heat that was still around and in them.

I remember, we had our first Galah (that was a pink and grey parrot) named 'Bimbo' in a cage at "Green Acres". One day, we hung his cage up in the shade of the huge great mulberry tree out the back. Later in the day, when we went to see what he was squawking about, we found him covered in mulberry juice where the mulberries had dropped into his cage. He had eaten them, then rolled over in them, it was odd to see 'Bimbo' staggering around drunk on the juice poor thing!

'Bimbo' used to love being talked to and talking back to us. His bird talk of squawking could really go on for a while, so one day I recorded him on an audio tape. Then we played it back to him another time, he thought it was great.

My neighbour came unexpectedly knocking on the door one morning after dropping her children off at the local school and asked what I wanted her for. I said that I didn't, so she asked why I called out to her as she was going home. We laughed when we realized that it was 'Bimbo', who had been calling out 'Hello' in an English voice, (mimicking mine) as she had been going past our front gate!

That year I put over 50lb of mulberries from that one tree into the freezer. I also gave lots away. We ate many of them ourselves and also cooked numerous pies and made jam from them during the season. That was the only tree the children were allowed to climb and hide in, they thought it was great; it was the biggest mulberry tree we had ever seen.

The neighbour who came when 'Bimbo' called out was the one who asked if she could feel my face. She was a young mum with children and I thought that it was an odd thing to ask. So she explained that as I was fresh out from England she wanted to touch my 'English rose' complexion. She then suggested I should keep it in good condition, and put moisturiser on before going out each day, as the harsh sun and wind in Australia would ruin my skin by drying it out. It was good common sense because I had stopped using makeup after arriving here, as the weather was so hot. I have been putting baby lotion on my face ever since, when I have washed it each morning. So I am very blessed to have quite good skin even now that I am in my 70's. I do try to tell the young ones (teenagers) in the family, when they start experimenting with cosmetic's. Also I say to them that it is a good idea to wash one's face before going to bed, as it gets rid of the dust that may have accumulated on the skin during the day. Oh! well, we can but try to help.

We erected an above the ground swimming pool, quite a large size, on the orchard property. One weekend, on a hot day a friend and I were in it with about six children, when we started to feel dizzy, feeling the whole pool full of water starting to move and collapse around us. We all got out very quickly as the water started pouring over one edge and the sides were caving in. We had not realised the importance of digging at least partway down into the ground to anchor it, so it was not quite as level as we thought. Never mind we learn by our mistakes, that's how some of us know so much - it's because we make so many mistakes. Well, no one was hurt, thank goodness and we all had a good laugh but the pool was not put up again! We all got used to using the dam to swim in further up the orchard.

While living at "Greenacres", I bought Pat a greyhound for his birthday and decided that I would like one for myself as well, so we chose two, a boy for Pat and a girl for me. 'Skippy' and 'Lady' we named them. For their track names, we chose 'Sawyers Boy' and 'Sawyers Girl'. They both did very well. 'Skippy' was a nice light brown, brindle colour and 'Lady' was similar, only a grey colour. They were quite big greyhounds. We trained them ourselves in the orchard, but not with live bait. Pat and I made a good job of training them, as they usually came in first, second or third when we raced them on the track at Cannington in Perth. Although we were offered big money for them, we brought them with us when we moved to Carnarvon in the North of Western Australia; we couldn't bear to leave them behind because by then they were part of our family. They were beautiful pets and used to come and make themselves comfortable indoors. They were supposed to be guard dogs, but I think we spent most of our time guarding them!

While Nanna Tainton was staying with us we used to take her along with us and the children to the Cannington track to the training sessions. We sometimes took a picnic, because we had to wait our turn for the greyhounds to race around the track. The children used to sit or stand on top of our station wagon to watch them run. It was a good time getting out for the day with the children and Nanna who used to enjoy those outings.

Then the time came to leave the orchard as, it was too wet and cold during the winter months for us in Sawyers Valley, especially Matthew and myself. So we decided to move further north. But where to? So we looked on the map and decided that it could be Carnarvon.

Chapter Thirteen

Carnarvon

We had thought of going on to a sheep station. So we went to the real estate office for an interview regarding doing this. We needed to know what was involved. Well, the agent asked us if we had any experience with sheep? We told him 'yes', we had. Then he asked "how many"? He nearly fell off his chair laughing when we told him – three. Then acting facetiously looked at me and asked, "what were their names dear"?

Yes, we did know that on the stations there are thousands of sheep and no, we had never lived on one. Well, we had only been out from England about a couple of years at that time but had read up about life on sheep stations here in Australia, so we thought we would be able to manage one, but only if we had another family on there with us.

We had friends who thought about being partners with us but they changed their minds, eventually they went back to England to live. Years later, we visited them when we went over to the U.K. and they said they always regretted not making the effort to go with us onto the sheep station. What put them off was the experience they had when they went to view the station.

This is what had happened. First of all, Pat and myself went to look and inspect the property one weekend. The station owners were very good to us, having a lovely meal, lots of water plus cool drinks prepared for the evening meal when we arrived. We were hot, tired and dusty from the long over twelve hour drive from Perth. We had Ruth and Matthew with us and as it was getting dark in the early evening, we had to wait until morning to look around. It was lovely. The homestead was within walking distance to the beach, where I stayed for a while with the children, while Pat was taken for a windmill run around part of the property.

After returning home to Perth, we then reported back to Alice and Dave, suggesting they should check it out for themselves before becoming business partners with us.

So, they drove up to view the property on the next weekend taking their three children with them. When they got as far as Geraldton they thought they were nearly there, not realizing that they were not even half way, so they had to continue to drive on to Carnarvon. Remember they had not long emigrated out from England like ourselves and didn't know that there was such a great distances between places in Australia.

They arrived in Carnarvon after travelling about twelve hours or more from Perth. From Carnarvon town they phoned the sheep station for more directions and found that they had about another couple of hours driving on unmade roads. Well, on one of the narrow sandy roadways the sand moved their car over to one side and they were bogged. Now at that time they were in over forty-degree heat, late afternoon. They had set off from Perth in the early hours of the morning, so were very tired, very hot and Alice was getting very tearful. They had to put grass and branches under the tyres to try and dig themselves out. Then the car would not start, they had run out of water! They then put their drinking water into the engine (or wherever they needed to put it) not having enough water they put in their orange drink as well. It took them so long that the station people sent out a search party to find them.

The search party from the station were very good; they helped to get the car moving and drove back to the homestead, with our friends and children following quite slowly on the unmade roads. Eventually they got there in the dark. The lady of the house had a lovely meal ready for them, after the meal they went over to stay in the cottage which had been made ready for them to stay in overnight.

Alice said that during the night she could hear a swishing sound. They didn't know that the cottage they were sleeping in was on a cliff quite near to the ocean. It was dark when they had arrived so they had no idea regarding the landscape of the place.

Because she was frightened of the desolation and wildness of the sheep station they kept the lights on in the kitchen all night. She also said that she kept her head under the bedcovers because a bat had flown in and things kept flying around. Apparently, they were huge great moths being drawn in by the light, so in the morning the walls of the kitchen and ceiling were covered with hundreds of them. Alice kept a scarf over her head; some were as big as or bigger than a tea plate. We had previously seen them when we had stayed there and thought they were beautiful.

After breakfast, Alice, Dave and the children were taken for a walk down to the beach, also to a look around the property. It was not the best day of the year for them to pick. If you remember, there is sometimes, a day in the year, that the flies seem to come out. Well, that was the day! Mostly they kept flying around Alice's head. We realized afterwards that it was because she had an ear infection at the time and that was why they were buzzing around her more so than the others. The back of her clothes were black with hundreds of small flies, she just could not stand it and thought maybe it would be like that all the time. But of course, it isn't, there is just that one day a year when there seems to be more flies around.

There was not a blade of grass in sight because there had been no rain for quite a long time, hardly any trees to be seen apart from right near the house, it was a very, very dry property. Our friends (would be partners) had gone there thinking it would be beautiful and green similar to the coast in Ireland where they had come from. So they were not impressed!

When they came back to Perth they were quite distressed, apologising to us that they could not possibly live there. We were very disappointed as we just loved the place, although it was so vast and dry, the coast line and beaches with their soft sand and clear blue waters were truly beautiful. Pat and myself were not sure of going onto such a property without partners or helpers so we had to back off. Never mind these things happen!

After some consideration we decided to sell the orchard and come to Carnarvon to rent a property, until we could find something that we would like to run as a business. Well, what a carry on. Pat's parents were staying with us at the time we were moving, so they came from Sawyers Valley to Carnarvon with us. There was not enough room in our car for everyone, so Pat's father came up in the removal van with the furniture. We left Josephine with a family in Sawyers Valley on a small holding so that she could carry on her schooling at Governor Stirling High School. (Sad to say that decision was one of the worst decisions we ever made, leaving her with that particular family).

However, to press on with our story. Pat, plus his mother, myself, Ruth and Matthew drove up in our old Holden station wagon with a trailer on the back. In the trailer, we put our two greyhounds, the parrot in its cage, plus the children's cat's, 'Bubbles', 'Whisky' and 'Gingin', also some extra cases. Then, at the comfort stops, animals had to be fed and watered enroute. Because of all the weight in and on the car, it took about fourteen hours to get to Carnarvon.

So we arrived at Carnarvon in 1975, renting a house in Crossland Street while we looked around for a business to buy. While the children were at school during the day, Pat's parents came around with us to look at different properties until their holiday with us came to an end and it was time for them to return home to England. After a while living in Crossland Street, we eventually decided to buy a Plantation on South River Road which we named 'Larman Plantation'.

Chapter Fourteen

Plantation Days

Not knowing anything about growing bananas we very quickly had to learn or we would have gone broke. The Carnarvon Research Station people were very helpful towards us and we became good friends with some of them and still are. We lived on the plantation for over seven and a half years. It was hard work and I was very ill most of the time. However, eventually we did make a go of it.

When we first started and after not getting any returns from the market for the first six weeks we phoned up to ask where our cheques for the produce had gone? The market advisors said that our bananas had to be thrown out, as they were no good for sale. We said that we did not understand as they were in good condition when they were packaged and left the plantation. In those days there were no refrigerated trucks from Carnarvon to Perth, so produce was transported overnight, a twelve hour journey to the Perth markets. We had packaged beautiful large bananas some ripe and some nearly ripe, so of course they had become overripe on the trip down due to the gas that they emit in the boxes. So in the heat of the vehicle travelling down they had almost cooked. The market advisor suggested that we get professional advice from the Carnarvon Research Station or we would go broke. So Pat sent me to their office to get better instructions than those we thought we knew.

Well, they came around, called us 'Poms' and laughed their heads off at what we had been doing. Apparently, the bananas had to be green when they were packaged to send off. They thought it was a great joke that we had even sent yellow ripe bananas. Not only that, but when we washed them in the bath of water, we had used a small scrubbing brush to clean them. The men laughed even more when we told them that, because unknown to us at the time, every mark will show when they ripen, so bananas need to be treated like eggs (very carefully). Ours would have ended up with scrubbing brush marks on them when ripened! After they finished laughing, they then introduced themselves, had a beer with Pat and instructed us very well.

Our deliveries to the market improved so we looked forward to receiving our cheques.

The bananas on the outside of the rows of fruit were grown to protect the main body of bananas, so usually were very small and no good for market. The Research Department were trialling a new venture by using blue plastic bags to cover bunches of bananas, hoping to develop better fruit. We were one of the first plantations to experiment (with their instructions). Our decision was to put blue plastic bags on the outside of the rows to save them from being mainly useless. Well, we were so pleased with the results that we started to cover more bunches hoping to produce excellent produce, as the outside ones under the bags were even better than some of the main crop. After a time our bananas were top grade and were well sort after in the Perth markets often being spoken for before they reached there, also attracting top prices. It does pay to really listen to and receive instruction instead of trying to think we know best when we are new comers to any business that we try to work at.

'Larman Plantation' was another of our renovating properties, having to live in it while we built the house around the old place that only had two liveable rooms. Everything that had wings or could crawl or walk used to come into the house because there were no fly wires or doors that would shut properly. Some things we had never previously seen, blue tongue goanna's, snakes, centipedes, huge moths, stick insects, millions of ants, mosquito's, worst of all the huge cockroaches which used to fly around as well as get into the cupboards.

Regarding materials for our new house, we chose dark red clinker bricks. We had archways in the kitchen and lounge room; ending up with five bedrooms, large kitchen plus a large lounge room with built in corner seats, incorporating storage underneath. We also built another good sitting room and a small hallway.

But building the house was another drama. We decided to build around the old house, adding onto the two good brick rooms that were there, keeping the old kitchen to use until we could build a new one. Having got the trenches dug out for the footings and the metal frame work and roof span up, it started to rain. Well, it rained and rained, tropical hard down pouring torrential RAIN! It ran down like a waterfall from the two brick rooms the previous owner had built, into the kitchen because they had not connected the roof of those good brick rooms to the old kitchen. The old tin roof on the kitchen leaked all through onto the floor which was mostly unsealed, resulting in a lot of mud to walk in. Sometimes we could hardly hear each other speak because of the noise the rain made on the tin roof.

We used every container that could hold water to catch the rain as it came dripping or pouring in. Planks of wood were put inside the kitchen as walkways to the doors, so that we could fill the wheel barrows, walk them along the planks, tip the water outside, refill the wheel barrows over and over again from the containers collecting water ready to walk the planks again.

So, there we were - inside with raincoats on. One good thing we could say was that the rain was not really too cold, which was a relief as it continued for a few days. It was dreadful, Praise The Lord our beds were dry in the good two brick rooms. The electricity was attached to a post in the kitchen. All the wires ran from this particular point, which we somehow kept dry or it would have blown up, as there were wires hanging all over the place. The wires also went out somehow through the back door or windows to the sheds.

When everything had dried out we decided to have ready mix concrete poured for the floors. Well, the day the ready mix truck came churning cement as it drove down the long drive way, the noise frightened the big white horse that we had in the corral near the front of the house, so it jump over the top of the corral and bolted. Eventually, it was found and brought back home.

After a few days, the next lot of ready mix cement was poured for a couple of floors. We decided we could do these ourselves without the help of brickies. One of the rooms was going to be a bedroom for Matthew and we were also including a small hallway leading to the front door located between that bedroom and ours.

To speed things up we remembered that there was a smoothing machine the previous owners had stored in our share farmers quarters. The machine was one that the Italians use to make those lovely smooth red shiny floors with, which were there in the two good brick rooms when we bought the place. The machine had blades underneath similar to a lawn mower, you held the handles, pulled the string to start the engine, (which we had put fuel into), then it was supposed to smooth the cement to leave a lovely surface. Pat had a go, then it stopped. Then when we got it going again, it got away from him and went round and round, back and forth until it ran out of fuel. As it was going round and round it was digging a hole through the cement. We just could not get hold of it to stop it. I sat down and laughed and laughed. Pat was not amused. Eventually, we managed to get in touch with the brickies to come and help us. We had to put lights up so they could see as the day had disappeared on us. They were not happy because we had made such a mess of things and they had to work quickly before the cement set. Thank goodness they made a good job of smoothing the floors.

When the bricks were delivered for the main part of the house, we had asked the driver to come along South River Road, then down our long driveway to the front of the house because we had had so much rain. However, the driver thought he knew best and travelled along the North West Coastal Highway coming in through the back of the plantation with a great big truck. So, yes, he got stuck in the mud down the track at the back end of the property. The driveway was one mile long from front to back, once more Pat was not amused as he then had to organize men and tractors to get the truck out, which needless to say took all day. In all this we were still trying to run the plantation, take children back and forth to whatever, as well as serving tourists. The driver had to unload the bricks next day, he was not very happy either but some people can't be told, they seem to do the opposite of what you say when you try to warn them and wonder why they get into bother. Then we all have to help them get out of the mess they land themselves in. We were very thankful that we had good neighbours and helpers at the time.

When the brickies had bricked up to windowsill level, the windows were lost in transit for six weeks. While waiting for the windows to come we had more games and trauma with more rain. The dogs and cats used to run in and out of the half built house as there were not any doors attached at that stage. We had chosen rough dark red clinker bricks for the inside of the main living area's for a nice change. Well, one day 'Skippy' (our large greyhound) was running through the hallway, caught the fur on one side of his leg, which then split showing the flesh underneath. It was quite a large gash needing treatment and stitches straight away. We took him to the vet who then took us to the Carnarvon Hospital into the operation theatre. He laid the dog on the operating trolley to sedate and stitch up the fur on him. This would never be allowed now, but there was nowhere else to take him. It seemed a very odd wound because there was no blood as the flesh had not been broken, just the skin. Well, the vet stitched 'Skippy' up and thankfully everything healed up alright.

After all this we did end up with a really good house, one of the best at that time along the river but I have no great urge to build in Carnarvon again.I wonder why? Three of the new bedrooms were not clinker bricks, so we let the girl's paint their own bedrooms. They couldn't wait until the ceilings were in before wanting to sleep in them. We did have the roof on, so in they went. In the middle of one night there was a big scream from Josephine as a large blue tongue goanna fell from the roof onto her head while she was sleeping. It disappeared somewhere so we thought it must have run outside because we had no bedroom doors built on at the time.

About six weeks later there was another scream during the day, as she had to get things out from under the bed ready for the electrician to work in her bedroom. There was the goanna; it had made itself comfortable under her bed amongst the toys...toys, which should not have been under her bed in the first place. So after realizing that she had been sleeping in the bedroom with a goanna under her bed for six weeks you would have thought that would have been a lesson to keep ones room tidy! But, Oh dear, it does not work like that with teenagers! However, it was lovely to have her back living at home with us after she had been at school boarding out in Perth for quite sometime.

Out the back of the house we had built a good verandah and patio the whole length of the house. Also we built a large below ground swimming pool. That was the second pool Pat dug out by hand, remembering the one he did at "Gayhurst" in England. This one was also very big, running parallel with the back of the house. What we decided to do was to concrete the bottom and sides of the pool. All this had to be reinforced with wire mesh to hold the walls straight and to line the bottom, before the cement was poured in and smoothed over. So what happens on the day, yes, it started to rain, what a mess! The ready mix concrete truck came, churning the concrete around, so we had to make a start getting them to pour the concrete onto the floor. Thank goodness the rain stopped so that it could be completed.

After the floor was finished we had to wait a few days for it to set before concreting the sides. Again it started to drizzle with rain. We were very fortunate having good helpers to work with us to complete the sides by smoothing the concrete, bonding it over the metal mesh. With the helpers, it did get finished in the one day. But was a lot of hard work as it was a very big pool.

Before the pool was filled with water I painted an outline of a shark at one end. Well, it was quite scary at first when the pool was filled with water because with the movement of the water, when anyone was swimming it looked quite real as if it was moving. The pool water was kept the natural colour so that it looked green like river water and the sides and bottom were just the natural concrete, no blue liners.

The children used to climb up the big old berry tree (Cape Lilac) and jump off the branches into the deep end. It was very well used during the heat of the summer. Pat and I used to go in late at night sometimes, when it was too hot to get to sleep, not having any air conditioners all those years ago in the house, just ceiling fans, so it was marvellous to get in to cool our bodies. Also, it was nice to look up at the night sky and all the stars while floating in the cool pool water.

I remember it took a quite a while to fill such a large pool, so my friend, Ann, and I put our plastic chairs at the shallow end, and sat with our bathers on with our cold drinks and magazines to watch the water gradually fill the pool. We set a raised walkway around the edge of the pool to sit on, using pavers to match the verandah colours.

Pat built walk-in bird aviaries around three sides of the pool, they were about 3 metres wide. They contained different kinds of birds, mostly parrots. Then we had to get a bird license of course to keep them, they were all beautiful. We started off with a couple that could not fly very well, large white corella's, then built up the aviary with pink and grey galah's, green twenty eight's, rosella's and weero's. Pat used to go in to feed them and let them land on him for food. I was not game to go in after being pecked a few times, as they bite very hard.

Just near the gates to the pool we built an outside laundry with toilet and shower facilities, mainly so the children did not have to run through the house to the inside bathroom dripping wet. It was a lovely home when we eventually had it finished. While we were living and working on the property Pat partitioned part of the huge great shed for me to use as an art gallery. Previous to that, we had been using one of the rooms in the house but found it very inconvenient to invite people in to view paintings. The art gallery was the length of the shed which was forty foot long, we made it nine feet wide, then lined it all with peg board so that it would be easy to hang paintings just where we wanted them.

This was the first art gallery in Carnarvon, which we declared open in January 1977. It was very popular and I was kept busy with my paintings. There was an official opening of the gallery, which was advertised as a "Grand Opening by Mr. Mason and Exhibition by Jessie Larman, Joy Harding and Kit Keddie". Joy and Kit were Perth artists, whom I had met the previous year on an artist's coach tour. We became very good friends.

They were both a lot older than myself and very helpful in regard to the art world. After the opening, we had many tourists and dignitaries visiting it. Some tourist buses carrying forty passengers used to come and view the paintings plus craft work or to tour the plantation and to buy bananas. The art gallery was certainly a very popular addition to the town of Carnarvon.

Another attraction was the electric train set that Pat put in the big shed; he worked it out so that he could stand in the centre with the trains travelling around at table top height. It covered quite a large area. We made miniature stations and painted parts of the table top to resemble paddocks, then stood toy farm animals around. Where the main table top was attached to one wall I painted a large mural from the ceiling to the table top of sky with mountains, railway lines and a train on it.

Pat and I were the first people in Australia to make chocolate coated bananas. These we also sold to tourists as well as selling normal bananas. We were able to swap bananas for fish from people, who were holidaying in Carnarvon, so that we always had a freezer full of fish to eat.

Talking about chocolate coated bananas, Gavin Mason, who was then manager of the Tourist Bureau at the time, phoned to say he was bringing Tammy Fraser, the wife of Malcolm Fraser, the Prime Minister at that time, out to buy one. Well, I thought he was joking, so carried on with my cooking. Around about lunchtime I had my hands in the bowl, mixing flour and margarine to make a cake, when Gavin suddenly appeared at the kitchen door saying 'Jessie, hurry up, Tammy Fraser is here'. So out I went with my apron on, still not believing him, wiping my hands on a tea towel and yes, there she was! I must say she was very gracious, looking at me in my flour covered apron. (I felt a right 'narna'). So I finished wiping my hands and served her with a chocolate coated banana, which she insisted paying her dollar for. Well, I was in real trouble afterwards from Gavin, firstly for not believing him and secondly for letting her pay the one dollar.

Later that afternoon I realized that my engagement ring was missing from my finger and was hoping it had not come off in the cake mixture, that by then was made into a cake and was in the oven. Then I had a bright idea that it may have come off while serving Tammy Fraser as my hands were being wiped so quickly on the tea towel. So out we went to look on the ground, not holding out too much hope amongst the gravel by the place where we sold produce and the chocolate coated bananas. I stood and prayed that we could find it and was so thankful that we did because as you know engagement rings are really precious.

At one time someone offered us goat meat for our dogs in exchange for bananas, we said yes please, not realizing that they meant real live meat i.e. goats, until the day arrived that they brought them around. They tied them up to the horse corral, took their bananas and went. Later, when Pat came back from taking Matthew to play cricket, the men had long gone. Pat was not amused because we were not used to having goats. So we tied one up down the river, which by the way was just across the road from the front of our driveway. The Gascoyne River is usually a dry river bed in Carnarvon with the water running below ground. All plantations have a pump house on the bank of the river with wells sunk down into the sandy riverbed to pump up water from below.

Back to the goats. The next one, we tied up near my studio, which was half way along our driveway and the other goat around the back of the house. My studio, by the way, was the old share farmer's cottage. It was falling to pieces, not good enough to live in but excellent for me and the children to use for painting and other craft work that we were happy to do. I used to have adult students to teach now and again. Matthew and myself used one corner for making plaster models to paint, so that corner was covered white with polyfilla, plaster of paris as well as various rubber and plastic moulds. Also we had the tumbler set up in there for tumbling stones for the jewellery, that Matthew helped me to make using the stones that we collected from the river bed.

Around the back of the house near the swimming pool, we had chickens in a large covered enclosure. We used to let them out to eat the Turpentine Mango's when we were first there as we could not get used to the strong Mango taste. After a time though I got used to them, eventually getting to really like eating them. Pat however and the rest of the family were not too keen to eat those. There did not seem to be much market for that particular type of mango apart from selling them for chutney making. Yes, I learnt to make really good chutney with them. Also I might add that we collected a lot of banana recipes and made some good meals out of the banana's that we could not use for market. The beautiful purple banana flower can also be eaten as can most of the plant including the stem, which is of course is about ninety percent water. One particular lady used to come to purchase just the flower to use in her cooking.

We decided to make the chicken run (which was the size of a small shed) into a shade house for plants so that Matthew could learn about planting seedlings, which he enjoyed as well a being in charge of the chickens and eggs. It was an old wooden structure, held together with bits of tin, shade cloth and other odd things but it did have some tin over the top for a roof. The laying boxes were at one end plus perches for the chickens. We put planks of wood for plant stands down the centre. It was very rustic looking but we were happy with it. The chicken run even had a door to shut the chooks in at night. Well, what more can a young child ask for?

I can tell you a bit more of life on the plantation. Like I mentioned earlier, first we only had Ruth and Matthew with us there, as Josephine was at school in Perth. Ruth and Matthew went to East Carnarvon Primary School. Ruth finished her schooling at Carnarvon High School, leaving to go to work in one of the banks in town. Oh! I forgot to tell you that the girls had horses on the plantation and both belonged to the pony club in town. Ruth especially won many ribbons for dressage and cross-country riding. She used to get me to plait the horse's mane, then to plait her friend's horse's mane as well. It was quite a chore for me to do this at about 6 am standing on a crate or something to reach the mane's at the pony club grounds. It was mostly freezing cold at that time of the day during winter months.

Pat on the roof of the plantation house

Matthew was never very enthused with horses apart from helping to feed them or look for them when they went missing. Probably because one of them reared up so that he slid down it's back falling hard onto the ground. Mainly he liked to ride around the property and down the river on the three-wheel Honda motorbike that we used for work.

It was a sad day when Ruth's horse 'Danny' went missing. It had a stone eye and used to get out whenever it could to run with others over to Brickhouse sheep station. Mostly, it came back or we would find it but Ruth was very upset of course when it never came back that last time. There was nothing we could do when it eventually went off with the pack on the station property.

One beautiful horse that she had was almost black in colour, was part Arab and very highly strung. Tourists came around one day saying that a young girl had been thrown off her horse and was laying somewhere near the front of our plantation along South River Road. They didn't like to move her and asked if we knew who it might be or could we phone to report it for them. We went to look and found that it was our daughter. Well, the young stallion had thrown Ruth off and bolted. It was blessing that she was wearing her hard hat, which we said was compulsory if she was going to ride. We eventually did find the horse plus all her quite new and expensive saddlery.

It was a good life on the plantation. We had caretakers living on there with us to give a hand. The lady would help me in the house, while her husband helped Pat to serve tourists, also showing them around, giving them a talk about banana growing. We have stayed good friends with some of the caretakers that came to work for us over the years.

Caretakers, Gwen and Alf were with us during the 1980 flood; they were in their caravan living on the plantation during their stay. The flood water came up the steps through the door to about one inch (i.e. 2.5cm) throughout their caravan. Although that does not sound much, it was enough to ruin carpets and seep up through cupboards ruining quite a lot of their belongings.

There was a lot of preparation for us to do before the flood came. Pumps in the pump house down the river had to be lifted as high as possible to start with. Then all furniture that we could move was put out onto the banana benches in the shed. We had freezers lifted up onto the benches, plus carpets out of the house, apart from the one in the lounge room, which was made of seagrass square's to give the house a tropical look. The whole of that carpet floated on the water, which came right through the house up to our knees. To walk across the room you had to put your foot on top of the carpet, press it to the floor before lifting the next foot up then down, if you see what I mean, what a mess!. The house we had built with a good concrete floor but it took weeks to dry out. The phone eventually stopped working as the connection was under

Larman Plantation, Carnarvon, Western Australia

water in the lounge room near the skirting board. Since then, we have had all phone or electrical plugs at least a metre off the ground level wherever possible.

It doesn't have to rain in Carnarvon to flood the town as the water comes down from the rivers further north, filling the Gascoyne River and all the low lying surrounding areas. Our plantation was not flooded to start off with from the front, where the river goes past but from the back along the North West Coastal Highway. That being lower ground, it came up through the back of our plantation covering our baby bananas with about nine foot of water; before making it's way up through the main body of banana's to the back of the house then through the back door. We, the family had spent the night on the roof, not wanting to evacuate so that we could hose the house and sheds out as the water receded.

That was quite a trauma.....there was Pat, myself, Ruth, Matthew, plus Ruth's fiancé, Guy, who decided to stay and help. Pat carried the two greyhounds 'Skippy' and 'Lady' around his shoulders, up the ladder to put them on the roof. Yes, it was a sloping roof on the house but we had the dog's beds already on there so they did not slip off. 'Scruffy', Matthew's puppy (a black long haired terrier) and three cats, were on the roof with us. It was a bit of a worry watching 'Scruffy' the puppy, who had a beautiful long black hairy coat, chase the cats around the edge of the roof until he could be stopped.

We had mattresses for our family, with tarpaulins to cover us just incase it rained, which Praise the Lord, it didn't. However, there was very heavy dew, so all got wet anyway. I had a gall bladder attack during the night and had to climb down the ladder, a bit scary in the dark, to go indoors during the early hours to get some medication and phone for help. As South River Road was by that time flooded, it was decided I should wait until daylight to be evacuated.

Well, morning eventually came after what seemed to be a very long night with animals on the roof and the giggling engaged couple on the other side of the sloping roof. The sun came out and all seemed well, no flood yet through our house. We listened to the radio, which said the emergency seemed to be over and the town was saved. Well, they didn't reckon on us out on the plantations just starting to get wet. As we listened to the radio, we could hear an unusual sound; it was water lapping through banana's at the back of the house. It was something we could not stop, it just kept coming towards us, we quickly climbed the ladder back up to the roof and watched as the water came around the house, covering the swimming pool and filling our driveway.

So, I sat on the roof and did my knitting surrounded by family plus our animals. The horses we had previously taken to higher ground somewhere, as no, they would not have fitted on the roof! Well, sitting there, doing my knitting, waiting for some of the research station men to come with a small boat to evacuate Gwen, Matthew and myself into town, I found myself looking at the banana shed which we had renovated a few years earlier. Suddenly, it came to me that we had re-roofed that with a flat roof just incase we needed to get up high if there was a flood. With all the work that was going on to get ready we had completely forgotten this and had spent the night sliding about on the house roof! Oh well, we can't be bright at everything can we?

While we were evacuated, Pat, Ruth, Guy and Alf all stayed on the plantation to hose the house and sheds out with high pressure hoses to get the red river mud off of the walls. About one metre high it came through the art gallery, sheds and knee high through the house. While this was happening, the television crew came around with Sir Charles Court, showing photo's of the inside of our house, as I was still evacuated I missed out on that bit of excitement.

Other things that happened while we lived there were:-

1) Cyclones: The first one was not long after we had moved in and I remember we all huddled on our bed in one of the good brick rooms waiting for the cyclone to pass. Coming from England we were not sure what to expect, but we had good advice from our neighbours, Cate and Roger Veen, which we did listen to and were grateful to them for it.

2) Sandstorm: That was incredible to see (or not see), the sky starting to darken. When we looked up we saw this big storm cloud coming towards us in the distance, it was huge and threatening, it seemed to fill the whole of the horizon. It took a few minutes to realize that it was a sandstorm. We rushed inside the house to close all windows and doors. It took quite a time to move over the town of Carnarvon. We had to put lights on to see indoors as it was nearly as dark as night everywhere. Never had we been in one before, it was eerie as it passed and left a trail of fine sand everywhere, even through the house, with the windows closed.

3) Earthquake: Yes, even in Carnarvon. One day I was sitting in an armchair in the kitchen, having a cuppa, when suddenly the chair and the cup in my hand felt funny and moved. The crockery in the cupboards clattered slightly. It really felt like the whole ground moved just for a few seconds. Thankfully nothing worse happened to our place.

After a while we realized that the time had come for us to expand our chocolate coated banana business. Finding that it would have been too expensive for us to build a small factory on our property, we thought it best to move. We had been approached to send and service a supermarket in Perth city with the chocolate coated banana's. But with not much freezer transport, at that time from Carnarvon to Perth, which is one thousand kilometre's south, it would have been very difficult to service them.

So we decided to sell our plantation and move to Perth. At that time, our caretakers were an older couple, Daphne and Bill Williams. They were a great help while we were packing up to move. They just loved living on the plantation with us and we became good friends. We kept in touch over the years, which was quite easy as they moved back to live in the Perth hills, not too far or us all to visit them. Both have now gone to Heaven.

Chapter Fifteen

Forrestdale

In 1981 we moved back to Perth, where we bought a house to live in at Forrestdale. It was a big old house that had been looked after very well, including an acre and a half of land. There was an above the ground swimming pool with a raised sun deck with seating around one side of it. The back door led to a really lovely large patio. We put a pool table in the big shed and made ourselves quite at home, it was a lovely property. There were stables for horses and also a small pond down the back. Out the front of the house and to the side were lovely big lawns.

Matthew decided he would like a couple of ducks and a drake. They produced eggs plus ducklings and I came home from the factory one day to find him floating in the pool after school on a car inner tube with ducklings, plus 'Scruffy' dog in the pool with him. Not a good idea!

Another time we wondered why everywhere was covered with baked beans. Well, he had tried to heat them on the B.B.Q., which was on the back patio not realizing that you needed to open the can first...therefore it blew up! Then we found a bullet hole in his bedroom window. Well, after joining the rifle club, apparently he decided to practise, another not very good idea. It was there, in Forrestdale, that he bought his first car for $1.00. No, it could not be driven, but was a good status symbol sitting out the back to practice taking it to pieces. Probably, this helped him decide to be a mechanic.

At first he attended Kelmscott Senior High School and was able to receive a licence for a motorized scooter to travel there and back. To finish his schooling in Perth he attended Armadale Senior High School. From there, he was able to apply for an apprenticeship. He was very fortunate being accepted and having two to choose from one in Perth and the other in what he liked to call his home town of Carnarvon. He accepted and completed a four year apprenticeship back in Carnarvon at the Small Boat Harbour, to become a mechanical fitter. This necessitated going to Tafe College for study in Carnarvon and the practical exams in Perth once or twice a year. Well, enough about Matthew for now, so I will carry on with our story.

We lived there in the Forrestdale house while setting up our

Forestdale House in Perth

chocolate coated banana factory at Maddington. We had to design the interior of the factory, adhering to the government rules, which required stainless steel utensils and special blue coating for the flooring. Most of the work we did ourselves in setting it all up. It was a blessing that Pat's trade was a plumber because we needed sinks, troughs and drainage. In the factory we made the chocolate coated bananas, selling them through deli outlets, a Foodland Store, Woolworth's and Cole's. We even exported some over east to Sydney. Special boxes were made for them to go into the freezer compartments to compete with ice-cream varieties in those shops. We employed six young people in the factory plus a full time driver for our freezer truck. Also we set up the office, which being a secretary, was my domain.

When we moved from Carnarvon to the Forrestdale house, we had left Ruth in Carnarvon. She was engaged to be married and was employed working in one of the banks there; so Ruth decided not to come to Perth with us. We organized with our friends, Annie and Geoff van der Platt's, for her to live in the flat at the back of their house in Robinson Street. Plans changed in regard to the wedding being in Carnarvon to being in St. Matthew's Anglican Church in Armadale. This was the nearest one to us in Forrestdale. It was the most beautiful wedding with friends coming from around Perth, also down from Carnarvon, plus others from some of the sheep stations where Guy had been working as a professional roo shooter. Also, Alice and Bruce Teede, (Guy's parents) came down for the wedding from Carnarvon. Our daughter, Josephine, and Robert, who by then had two children (Robbie and Kylie), our first grandchildren, came down from Geraldton. It was so lovely to see them all.

As it was not practical for Ruth to bring her horse down from

Carnarvon, we hired a man from the hills around Perth, who had a horse and carriage business catering for weddings, which he drove himself in his special top hat and tails. It was a really excellent wedding, with the bride and bridegroom leaving in the horse drawn carriage, taking them to have photo's taken in a private garden in Armadale. The garden had a small bridge over a stream in between the lawns, which provided a lovely setting for photo's. Later, we had a sit-down wedding reception at one of the best local restaurant's in Armadale with approximately sixty guests.

After the reception, when the bride and groom went to leave in their vehicle which some of their friends had decorated, the car would not start… why? Because the car had been lifted up so that the back wheels could not turn. Then with much laughter and man power, it was lowered to the ground for them to take off.

Quite a few visitors came to stay with us during the three years that we lived in the Forrestdale house. Some of whom were Pat's parents from England, plus a family friend, Dorothy, who travelled with them from Plymouth in Devon U.K. They were joined a few days later by Pat's sister, Delia, and her husband, Andy. We had a caravan for Pat's parents to stay in just out the back by the pool and the others we accommodated somewhere inside.

Pat's mother was ill when they came and after a while did not take her medication. So when I came home one day from the factory, Dorothy was at the front gate waiting for me and said they had left. Where had they gone? Well, she said she didn't know. I phoned Pat, who was still at work in the factory. He had no idea that they were thinking of leaving. He came home to find Dorothy in tears saying they had left her behind in a foreign country and she was not sure what to do.

Eventually, we managed to get her to tell us that they had phoned the Salvation Army to come and get them. We then phoned the Salvation Army people, who told us that the mother had said we didn't want them and were going to put them out. This of course was not true. We had spoken to Pat's father that morning, before we went to work, who told us that the mother had not been taking her medication for a mental condition and was upset because I gave her a colour blanket that she did not like. So she had hidden all the blankets that we gave them to use, in the caravan under the mattresses and father thought that they did not have any. It was very cold at night and had rained, so that did not help the situation.

When Delia and Andy arrived from England a few days later, we had to tell them what happened. They went to visit them in the Salvation Army home but we were not allowed to go. What a carry on. So, Dorothy stayed with us and managed to visit the parents a few times before the three of them had to leave to go back to England. Delia and Andy however, stayed with us for six weeks; they hired a car for travelling around as part of their holiday, like they had done a few years previously when they had visited us on the plantation in Carnarvon.

Another time, Auntie Muriel, also from England, came with her husband, Brian, and our friend Derek's mother, Dot. Derek and his wife, Carol, were living in Paraburdoo miles away up north. Derek drove down to take Dot to Paraburdoo, staying for a couple of days with us before taking her back for a holiday to stay with himself and Carol. He dropped Muriel and Brian off at Geraldton on the way to Paraburdoo to stay with their daughter, Mary, and her husband, Jeff. That was a six hour drive to Geraldton, then after staying overnight, Derek drove Dot for a couple of days to get her to his home.

Then back they all came after a couple of weeks to stay and holiday with us, until it was time for them to go back to England, because they found it difficult to cope with the isolation of the outback up north. Derek brought Muriel and Brian, from Geraldton on his way back down from Paraburdoo with his mother, Dot. When the day came for us to take them to the airport for their return flight to England, Muriel came rushing in at breakfast time saying that Brian had locked himself in the caravan out the back that they had been sleeping in. He said he wanted to stay here and would not come out. What a carry on, Pat had to break a window to unlock the door, so we could convince him to get ready and go back to England.

He looked so well after staying here basking in our lovely weather that he did not want to go back to the snow and ice that was in their home town of Wivenhoe, Essex. Well, he had to go home - so that was that!

We do seem to get a few traumas with our relations and visitors. Never mind eh! Looking back, it all adds interest to life even though a bit wearing at the time. But we are here to look after each other on this planet earth.

I should have told you that, while we had the factory we did take our food caravan to the Royal Show in Perth to sell the chocolate coated bananas. Pat, Matthew and myself manned it, so that was quite an adventure. Likewise another adventure was to take the tucker box van filled with chocolate coated bananas to the "Festival of the Trees" run by the

'Orange' and 'Flower' people. Pat drove us there with the tucker box on the trailer to set up for Matthew and myself to sell them, as he was too embarrassed to be seen with the 'Orange' and 'Flower' people. Never mind, it takes all sorts to be part of this world. I must say they were a lovely group of caring people. Mostly vegetarians with odd food stuffs selling on the day, it was a good Festival somewhere in Perth.

Processing banana's in our factory in Perth proved not to be a viable proposition, after a bad cyclone season in Carnarvon. It was then too expensive for us to continue purchasing bananas from the Perth market, where they had been brought in from other States. The purchase price went up really high, so we were not able to mark up our product to compete with other frozen confectionary in the supermarkets. Having no bananas to process we had to let our workers go. We decided to wind up the business, sell the house in Forrestdale to pay what we owed to the bank, pay the workers wages, sell the freezer truck and advertise and rent out the factory.

Then we rented a house for a while in Armadale, returning to

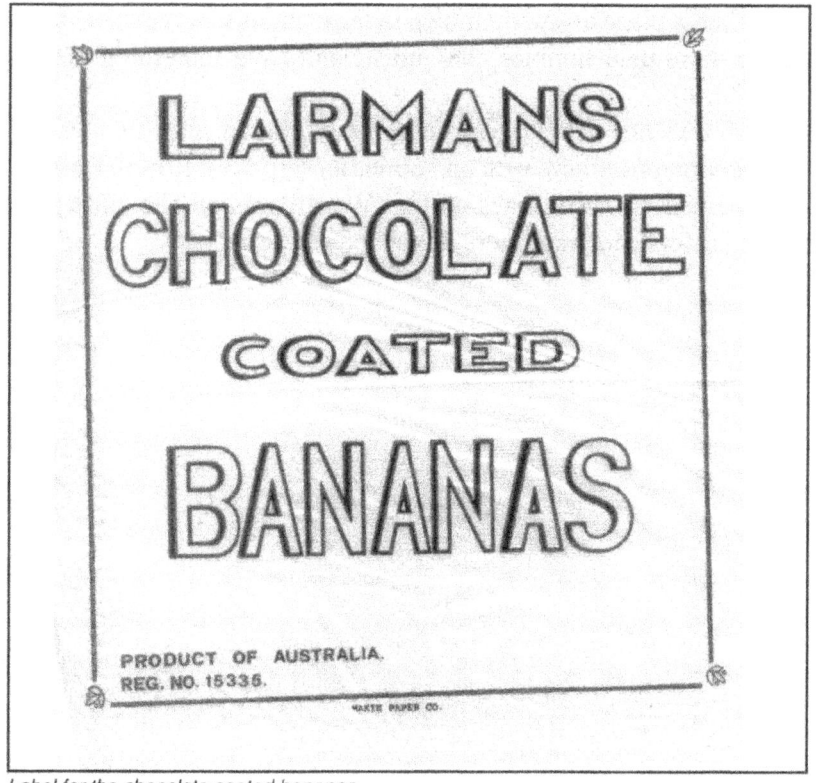

Label for the chocolate coated bananas

Carnarvon in 1985, where we been ever since. The house in Armadale, which by the way, was not far from Forrestdale, was very nice and was within walking distance for Matthew to get to the Armadale High School.

I remember one room being full of packing boxes because we had not decided what we were going to do. Well, then we had a phone call from a friend needing to stay with us, because she had an appointment to go to Fremantle Hospital. After her twelve hour journey, we picked her up off the bus. She always remembers her visit to us there as we had to set up a bed for her in-between the boxes. Next morning, we took her to hospital, where she was admitted for a few days before coming back to stay in the middle of the boxes again. Well, that was a different kind of visit. When she felt alright, we were able to put her on the bus for her twelve hour trip back home to Carnarvon. Yes, she did get better but I forget what was medically wrong.

Down the back garden, we allowed Matthew and his friends, teenage boys, to use one of the sheds as a den in the evenings instead of roaming the streets, it worked out very well. It was a good idea that the teenagers had a place to call their own in the evenings. Somewhere to invite friends to share their hobbies, play music and have something for supper to eat and drink.

Pat was not very happy being unemployed after us closing the factory, so when Matthew won an apprenticeship for a firm in Carnarvon, we all decided to come back home. We all missed the lifestyle that Carnarvon offers and were more than happy to come back.

Chapter Sixteen

Return to Carnarvon

One real estate agent asked if we would like to be caretakers for the lighthouse keepers cottage, by the one mile jetty. As it had been badly vandalized we would have had to buy a caravan to live in on site. That was out of the question as we were bringing about a houseful of furniture with us.

However, after a lot of phone calls it was very difficult to find a house to rent all those years ago and eventually we rented an old small house on George and Rosa Allen's plantation, just over the Gascoyne River crossing. It had not been lived in or looked after properly for a number of years. Before we moved back to Carnarvon, four of our friends cleaned it up – inside and out. They were a real blessing to us. We decided we would be living there, temporarily while looking around for somewhere else. However, we lived on that property for two and half years while trying to make a decision on what best to do.

The owners invited us to become share farmers, as there was a lot of land we could use but Pat declined this, thinking it would be best for him to try for nine to five employment. After being out of work for quite some time Pat started work at Carnarvon Regional Hospital as an orderly. Then when a vacancy became available for a maintenance worker, he applied and was accepted especially because his normal trade was as a plumber.

It was so hot in that little old house on the plantation, with no air-condition and no glass in some of the louver windows. While we were living there, I had a commission to paint a large oil painting, so I would set myself up about 6am on the front verandah, wrap myself in a thin wet sheet to paint a bit each day. In the kitchen, I painted a large mural on the wall above the kitchen table with a landscape painting and the ocean under the table. When the grandchildren, Kylie and Robbie, visited I let them paint on the wall under table which they thought was great, Robbie painted cars (he was good at that) and Kylie did fairies or something similar floating about in the water.

I was in a lot of trouble from their mother allowing them to do this, as they could not understand why she wouldn't let them paint on their own bedroom walls. I was asked not to teach the children silly things, but that is what grandparents are for.

Another time she brought them over for a hair cut. All went well with Kylie and Samantha but Robbie hid on the plantation. His hair had grown quite long and he wanted a prickle cut. Not having done a prickle cut, we found him and convinced him that, yes, Nanna could do that. So he sat holding a mirror to make sure I did it right, it had to be cut quite short and stand up on his head something like a crew cut, which I used to do for Pat. Well, Robbie was that pleased with his new hair style and couldn't wait to show his friends. I used to cut all the families hair until they became teenagers, then feeling grown up and with their own money they could go to the hairdressers. I had always cut Pat's hair for over 50 years, also my own.

While living there, Matthew was getting on with his apprenticeship at the Small Boat Harbour in Carnarvon. He was also enjoying fishing. I remember one evening very late, he arrived home pushing his bike with a fish larger than himself on it. Pat and I were in bed, so we had to get up and help him bring it into the laundry room; we had never had such a huge fish. Also he was sometimes out 'roo' shooting with his brother-in-law, Guy, and the other men.

It was good that Josephine, Robert and their children – Robbie, Kylie and Samantha, also Ruth, Guy and their son, Shaun were all living in Carnarvon when we came back here about 1983. Eventually, we decided to buy a house and settle permanently. Looking around, we found 23 West Street which would suit us. We bought it and have spent all the years since we moved in, renovating it. After a time, the shire decided to change the house numbers, so we are now 33 West Street, which of course, made it a nuisance to change the address on business cards, books, letterheads and my home occupation details for the Carnarvon Art Studio.

Yes, I am still painting, also teaching on the back patio once a week. The weather is so good, that we can paint outside for most of the year. I did go back to work as a secretary to the officer-in-charge of the Carnarvon Airport for a while because Pat wanted me to go back out to work. So I was very fortunate to find such interesting employment. However, that came to an end when the government of the day decided to close those departments around the state. Thankfully, that put an end to me going out to work and I could spend more time at home on computer work and oil painting.

I

33 West Street, Carnarvon 2013

remember while I was employed at the airport, one of my nephew's, named Kevin, who lived in England asked if he could come to Australia and stay with us for a holiday. When he came over, before he came to us he went to stay with his cousin, Josephine, and her family in Bunbury for a while. There was great rejoicing when they met up with each other because, living in the same village in England when they were younger, they had been going to the same primary school. They were both now in their late twenties and it was good to catch up on family news. Also Josephine and Rob's children thought their Uncle Kev was great. Eventually, he outstayed his welcome by not contributing financially each week and expecting to be waited on not lifting a finger to help. He would play with the children, spend time in the different pub's and loved talking to all the young ladies, who thought he was someone special. A real ladies con man, that was what Josephine realized. Then she decided after several weeks to send him up to us, because it looked like he did not want to move on and was making himself too comfortable in their home.

By this time Kevin, not working of course, had almost run out of money, so he could not afford the fare to get from Bunbury to Carnarvon. Josephine had the brilliant idea to make a placard and get him to stand at the end of the road going north. She felt very bad about this, but had enough of him sponging off her and her husband, Rob.

After picking the children up from school that day she peeped around the corner where she had left him, feeling awful that he was still there. She decided she would take the children home and if he was standing there late afternoon would have to pick him up and take him back to her house. Later when she went to check on him, he was not there, so he had obviously got a lift to come north to us. Josephine phoned me to say that Kevin was on the way and hopefully should be there the next morning.

Next day came and no Kevin, so we all start to worry where he was. The day after came and still no news. We decided to wait one more day just incase the driver had stopped overnight for a rest from driving, as it sometimes takes over fourteen hours to drive from Bunbury to Carnarvon. If he did not arrive on the third day we agreed to phone the police. No need to have worried, he arrived looking very pleased with himself, with not a care in the world. He had never given a thought to let us know that he was alright. Apparently, he had a great time camping overnight with the truckie in the outback. He said they lit a campfire, watched out for kangaroo's, slept in the open looking up at the stars in the vast night sky. Also he enjoyed being driven, seeing this part of the north of West Australia for the first time. Calling in at a couple of roadhouses on the way, the truckie had kindly bought him food and drink.

Well, there we are. We welcomed him and gave him a room in our house, saying that he could stay for a holiday with us for two weeks, after that he would need to pay for his keep, mainly for food, water and power. We didn't want to ask much from him just a little something.

Well, that would be "O.K." he said agreeing that he would look for work during the two weeks. But of course he did not. Pat used to get cross coming home for lunch or after work each day to find Kevin on the sunlounger spread out on the back lawn, basking in the sun to get a tan, then in the evening sprucing himself up to go out on the town.

In desperation to get him out of the house and into work, Pat found him a job helping with painting and decorating with a firm here. However, that did not last too long because he was a lazy worker. Not to be outdone, Pat took him to the Small Boat Harbour, to ask if they had a place on one of the prawn trawlers and, yes, they did. So we fitted him out with the necessary clothing and off he went. I think the contract was for about ten days or two weeks out at sea. When he arrived back he looked the worse for wear and staggered in the door in a great state. They had rough weather out on the ocean and he thought he was going to die, so he said that he even prayed, promising God that if He spared him he would come to church with me on the first Sunday that he would be back with us. Well, he didn't die thank goodness and yes, he did come to church to say thank you to God. Needless to say, he didn't seem to think he needed to come any more after that.

Anyway that was the end of that, which was just as well as my mother, sister, Jill, and her husband, Peter, were due to come from England and stay with us. But before they came, Pat and I were due to go on holiday so we invited Kevin to stay and look after the house for a couple of weeks, which suited him fine. On our way back from holiday we picked up Mum, Jill and Peter from Perth and travelled home.

Mum had to have Kevin's bedroom so he had to sleep in a swag on the floor in the studio. I went in to make up the bed in the room that he had been sleeping in and it smelt very fishy in there! Under the bed there was wet fishing gear, the mattress was wet and fishy where Kevin had put some of the wet stuff on. So, I found one of our blow up pool mattresses for Mum to sleep on. Next morning, she said she had not slept a wink because it deflated during the night and she could feel all the springs through it on the bed, poor soul she felt bruised all over.

Then we had to go out and purchase a new mattress as the other, which had been quite new, now smelt fishy and had to be thrown out. Kevin however, had not thought of reimbursing us. He was so over joyed to see Mum (who was his auntie) because she used to help look after him when he was younger. Can't tell you any more about Kevin at the moment, it gets too complicated apart from the fact that when Mum, Jill and Peter left after a couple of weeks, he decided to go to Broome to find work. A few weeks later he arrived back suddenly about 3 am stumbled through the door and told me he was in love. Well, as I had to get up to let him in I was not very amused and neither was Pat at being woken in the middle of the night. We just had to get him to go back to England. Back to something sensible.

Not long after the Kevin's episode, which had lasted best part of the year, my friend Marion, (who I was taking home for lunch) and I were coming home from church and called into the Hubble Street store for the Sunday Times newspaper plus something extra for lunch, when we smelt smoke. We could not see where it was coming from, so continued to drive to my home at West Street and found that it was cordoned off. At first we thought it was our house but no, it was the next door neighbours. We had to stop the car and walk along the roadway but were stopped from going through our gate by the fire crew. The neighbours were crying in the street and Pat was on our roof with the watering hose shouting for me to get inside and help, so reluctantly they let Marion and myself in through the gate.

Pat wet down all that side of the house, where next door was on fire, to stop it from spreading over to our place, especially as the gas bottles were there. It was a blessing that they did not blow up, while he was on the roof above with the hose turned on to them. Well, eventually the house fire next door was put out but it was not liveable anymore and had to be demolished. It was a Homeswest house, so thankfully, the people were able to be rehoused. After a while, a really good new brick house was built on the site of the burnt out one.

We had people come around in the afternoon to see how we were, that day of the fire, and they could not believe that our house did not smell of smoke or was blackened in anyway. Pat had most recently decorated through the kitchen, bathroom and laundry the week before the fire and it still looked good and fresh. I was able to tell friends that Marion and I had prayed for God to protect our house, and for His Holy Angels to guard it, and they had. It was incredible, even Pat could hardly believe that we had no smell of the smoke throughout the whole house even being so close to next door.

My Bible reading for the next day before I went to work was: "If your neighbour's house is on fire for The Lord, and yours isn't, then you should watch out". I read this out at work when we had morning tea and they were quite amazed. Praise the Lord for His protection for us. Nobody was hurt in the fire next door, all the children plus adults, although quite frightened and shocked were alright.

A bit more about 33 West Street

Pat and Matthew built a double garage at the back of the garden, not long after we first moved in. After painting, plus renovating the inside of the house, putting a spa bath in the bathroom and various other things to make ourselves comfortable, we then built a room along the back of the house, forty foot long to use as the art studio. Pat wanted me to keep it tidy, so he carpeted the floor and put peg board all around as an easy way for us to hang paintings up. We have had several art exhibitions here over the years and they have been very good.

Also after a few years we added a patio along the back of the studio, mainly to keep the hot sun off of the paintings. Later we put in a covered in swimming pool, therefore mostly filling up the back garden. The pool has spa outlets, one with a long seat with jets that allow bubbles to come through to massage you. There are jets at one end that we can swim against to help keep us keep fit. We use the pool cover to stop the water from evaporating too much. We also covered the roof with solar water filled hoses to heat the water and recycle it into the pool. This way we can get an extra couple of months use before winter sets in. After putting in the pool, we paved the driveway from the front gate, around the pool and around the house as well. I put a new front wall to replace the old fence at the front of the property in 2010, plus a new roof on the house in 2011.

As I said earlier, we moved into this house in West Street in March 1987. A couple of months later, in May, I went back to England to see the family for the first time since emigrating in 1973, that would have been 15 years since last seeing them waving us off on the train station in Colchester. I went on my own as Pat didn't want to go, then, at the last minute, he wished he was going, so he went the next year. Since that time, we both went back together for a visit. During those fifteen years quite a lot had happened in our family of course with the children growing up and also regarding myself.

I would like to add a bit about Pat here. Pat continued to work in the Maintenance Department of the Carnarvon Regional Hospital. Also for a good few years he continued to coach the young boys for soccer. He liked to play tennis and also chess. Pat accepted a redundancy just about the time of his 65 birthday. He was happy to retire from work, also from the soccer. He continued to do maintenance work around the town and play chess on Thursdays with a friend, while I was teaching oil painting here on our patio. He was still playing tennis once a week. He enjoyed having holiday's on the cruise ships and we were very fortunate to go on several different ones. During the year, 2006, Pat was diagnosed with Acute Myeloid Leukemia and sadly died on the 27th January 2007, aged 69 years. It was a very sad time for all of us.

Chapter Seventeen

Divine Healing

While on the plantation my health became progressively worse. At one time, I went to Perth on the coach thinking it would be the last time I would be able to travel. I stayed with my artist friend, Joy Harding, she encouraged me to go an iridologist, who put me on a diet of juices, saying that I had come to her too late for healing. She didn't think they would help me much but to give them a try, if I wanted to. By this time I was constantly on antibiotics and painkillers, my body had swollen up with bronchiectasis (similar to emphysema), coughing and bringing up sputum as the disease was ravishing both lungs.

Well, I took the diet back home to Carnarvon and started with all the vegetable juices. For about three days, I could hardly move my legs, but I was determined to keep trying with it and, yes, the diet saved my life at that time and put me in remission.

The diet was pretty awful to start with and I needed help to clean and juice all the vegetables. Matthew was very good at helping with scrubbing the carrots and pushing most things that were needed through the juicing machine. He would stand on a chair to reach at the sink as I could not stand long enough to do this, so that was a great help. The rest of the family also did their part to help in between their work.

From around nearly thirteen stone I went down to around under seven stone. Although, I went a yellow colour due to the carrot juice, I felt better and was off the antibiotics and then I started to come good. But sometimes things don't last and when we moved back to Perth in 1981, my health deteriorated again so I was back on antibiotics most of the time. A lady at church asked me to go for healing, which I knew nothing about at that time. But I know differently now. The main reason for writing this is to say, after coming to Australia I still had lots of ailments and I believe that The Lord Jesus Christ healed my lungs of bronchiectasis in 1984 in Perth, Western Australia by the laying on of hands at a Church service there. This now being the year, 2013, so it was a long while ago that I received my Divine healing. It was truly a miracle, as there is still no known cure for that disease.

Each year a notice used to come for the compulsory X-Ray that I was obliged to have since immigrating here to Australia. It was for a chest X-Ray because of the disease of bronchiectasis. That last time I had the X-Ray, I went in to see the doctor (he was a little Indian man) who asked me lots of details thinking that he had the wrong X-Rays for me. He went out to ask the nursing sister on duty, came back, asked me again what my name was and what I was there for. Also he asked what I had done since my last visit because the disease had disappeared out of my lungs and nothing shown up on the X-Rays.

The lungs were still scarred from all the pneumonia's I had had in the past but no bronchiectasis. He said he wanted to know what I had done, as it could possibly help other patients with the same problem because there was no known cure for that disease. So I told him that I had been on vegetable juices to help, he said that was good, but although they may put the disease in abeyance they could not have taken it away. So what had I done? Well, I told him that I had gone to church and had hands laid on for healing, asking him not to fall of the chair laughing! He said he believed me, as there was no other way I could have been healed except that God had done it. Now, he said "I want to make sure you are the person you say you are, what about your lobectomy, when did you have that done and where?" So I told him it was when I was about eighteen years old in the Royal Brompton Hospital in London, U.K. "Right," he say's "and who did the operation?" As it was so long ago I said I could not remember. Anyway, he said there was no hurry, just to sit still and think for a few moments.

Well, I thought and thought then remembered that the surgeon had a funny name something like Mr. Smelly. He was amazed and said he believed me because he trained under the surgeon Mr. Smelly in London, in the Royal Brompton Hospital, where I had the operation to remove the lower lobe from my left lung. This was incredible, a Divine appointment by The Lord. The doctor told me that I need never to go back for compulsory X-Rays, unless I had any worries about my lungs.

I Praise God for His healing power, the same now as when Jesus walked upon the earth 2000 years ago. Also I have come to know The Holy Spirit more fully in my life, hoping that The Lord God can use me for His work and Glory. The Holy Spirit is our teacher, comforter and guide. He wants us to fellowship with Him each day. He is the one who helps us to pray. His presence is lovely. Once you have lived with The Holy Spirit (who is The Spirit of Jesus Christ), you will never want to live without Him.

If anyone is reading this and is not a Christian and would like to become one, here is one way that you can do so. You could pray this prayer or a similar one: -

> *Dear Jesus, I know I am a sinner,*
> *I repent of my sins.*
> *Please forgive me and come into my heart*
> *To take charge of my life.*
> *I acknowledge God as my Heavenly Father,*
> *Jesus as my Saviour and I would like to accept*
> *Your Holy Spirit into my life.........Amen.*

If you pray the above prayer, and really mean it, you are immediately accepted by Jesus and are Born Again. Then you belong to the Kingdom of God. You need to tell a Christian that you have taken this step, to speak out is an action of faith and confirms that you have now become a Christian.

It would be good to read St. John, chapter: 3 verse 3 as a start. Then, begin reading the Bible each day, find a good Christian church and fellowship with other believers. You should remember that all the Saints in church, were sinners that have been saved; no one is born a Christian, we all have to make that decision for ourselves.

Going to church does not make anyone a Christian, no more than going to McDonalds or Hungry Jacks makes you into a hamburger. At the first opportunity, be baptized in water if you would like to be. Being filled with The Holy Spirit, once you have accepted Jesus as your Lord and Saviour, you may receive a heavenly language and speak in tongues, like it says in the Bible, but everyone does not do this.

There are many gifts that God blesses us with and we do not always have the same as our friends. It depends on what God our Heavenly Father wants us to use the gifts for. You will find a list in the Bible of the gifts in 1 Corinthians: chapter 12 starting at verse 4 if you would like to see what they are. No, you do not have to speak in tongues to be a Christian. But it is great when you can; also The Holy Spirit likes to sing sometimes in the Heavenly Language

To have a better understanding of the above , this is what I believe:-
Once you have Jesus in your life, the Holy Spirit is with you. Obviously, you can't have one without the other, because Father, Son and Holy Spirit are three in one, that is a Trinity (that means three) they are separate but

one. A bit difficult to tell you, but as you read the Bible you will begin to understand all truths because The Holy Spirit is our teacher, as well as our guide and comforter. Our body is a temple for The Holy Spirit to come and dwell in. The Holy Spirit dwells in the inner most part of our being.

When you invite Jesus into your life, you are saved and your own spirit will go to be with Jesus when your body dies. You need have no fear of death, because Jesus died on the cross for our sins. When you belong to him remember and know that Jesus is alive. He arose from the grave, ascended into Heaven; he came back, walked upon this earth and was seen by many people, especially his Disciples. You can read all these things in your Bible.

Many people are very happy to have invited Jesus into their lives. However, if we want to minister in the Kingdom of God here on earth, we really do need to acknowledge and to walk with The Holy Spirit in our heart. To fellowship with him each day (that means to talk with him) let him know that you appreciate Jesus and our Heavenly Father. Thank the Lord for all our blessings. The devil is real and we can only overcome our weaknesses with the love of Jesus being in us.

Once you have lived with God our Father, Jesus Christ, His Son and The Holy Spirit you would never want to live without them. Remember God is Love, before you were born He knew you, He wants you to be his own but He has given us freewill to choose either to love Him or to reject him. When we reject him, we must be aware that we are still in the devils Kingdom in the world but not in the Kingdom of God here on earth.

Other Healings:

I have received lots of healings for bronchiectasis, osteoporosis, cholesterol and arthritis. My arthritis is healed, (spirit of arthritis has gone.), ulcers healed and bones aligned. My heart more recently has received healing - so many healings and deliverances God has allowed me to have.

The Lord is amazing, He can heal anything, everything according to His will at the right time for us in our lives - especially if we truly try our best to walk with God our Heavenly Father, Jesus our Saviour, to fellowship and walk with The Holy Spirit (The Spirit of Jesus) all the days of our lives.

God is an awesome God, He loves us His own, with a fearsome love. He protects us with His Holy Angels and cares for our families and us because we are precious to Him. All who invite Jesus Christ, God's Son into their lives, belong to the one God above all God's - Our Father in Heaven. He is our Spiritual Father - the Father of Jesus.

When God becomes our Spiritual Father that makes Jesus Christ our Saviour, He is also our Brother as we become part of Gods family - that is, Brothers and Sisters in Christ. (Adopted Sons of the Living God) This is my belief.

Jesus is Lord.
St. John chapter 3 verses 15-16
That whosoever believeth in Him should not perish but have eternal life. For God so loved the world, that He gave His only begotten Son, that whosoever believeth in Him should not perish but have everlasting life.

Chapter Eighteen

Family Members

Some of our relations on Jessie's side of the family

My Grandmother Nanna Wyatt:

Nanna Wyatt

She was my fathers' mother. Her name was Rosina Wyatt, but the family used to call her Rose, and the younger ones called her Nanna Wyatt. She was a good lady, the one who tried to keep her big family together, when they were all married and not living at home, apart from her son, my Uncle Frank. She would walk a long way to visit them or go by bus. Sometimes, it would take her the whole day to walk to one of their houses, stay for a while and walk back home to cook Uncle Frank's evening meal.

She was left a widow at an early age with nine children to care for. I was told that she used to tie some of them to a tree in the garden while she got on with the washing. I don't know anything about her husband, Frederick George Wyatt (my grandfather), except that he was killed in the First World War.

Some of my Aunties and Uncles - my Father's Brothers & Sisters

Dad (my father) Ernest George Wyatt, was usually called Ernie. His brothers were: Frank,

Frederick George Wyatt

Jack (whose name was John) and Cyril William. Cyril was killed in action in the Second World War on 1st. May 1945. My brother, Cyril, was named after him and is said to look very much like my father and his brother, Cyril.

Dad's sisters were: Hilda, Lily, Margery, Winnie, Ena and Bessie. My father, Ernest Wyatt, was the youngest in the family. He married my mother, Jessie Emily Stebbings, when they were both eighteen years old and Mum was pregnant with me. They went on to have seven children: Jessie (that's me), Jean, Jill, Christopher, Cyril, Clive and Jasmine.

Frank Wyatt

Frank Wyatt never married. He courted a young woman for several years, but after finding out that she went out with someone else one evening, he ended the engagement. He mourned his lost love all his life. He lived at home with his mother, looking after her in her later years before she had to be institutionalised because of her erratic behaviour. When Frank died, he was buried in the same graveyard in Wivenhoe, Essex, where his mother and father and brother Cyril were buried.

Jack Wyatt: He married Truda. They had four children, June, Dawn and twins Pearl and Joy. I believe they all married. June was married to a policeman. Uncle Jack used to look for treasure in the bins. Large bins were put out along grass areas of the road. One day travelling in the car, my passenger said that there were feet sticking out the top of a bin as we drove past on the main bypass road. So I said to her "don't worry, it is most likely Uncle Jack looking for treasure".

Jack Wyatt and wife Truda Challis

Cyril Wyatt: He was killed in active service during the Second World War.

Cyril Wyatt

Hilda Wyatt: Married Mr. Nessling, who I believe was her first husband. He was run over and killed by a horse and carriage outside the Cross Inn, at Wivenhoe Cross, Wivenhoe while walking home from the pub in the dark. They had two children, Donald and Johnny, who both married and had children. Donald was married three times. Johnny still lives with his wife, Mary, in Wivenhoe.

Hilda Wyatt

Lily Wyatt: Married Claude Percival and they had one child, Brian, who married a young woman named Christine. Brian and Christine's first child at around two years old, died of cot death syndrome. I believe they had other children after that. Auntie Lily was one of my favourite aunts, who I used to visit now and again, when we lived in Wivenhoe. She was a Godly woman and used to teach Sunday school at St. Mary's Church in Wivenhoe. She had a motorized bicycle and used to ride it in all weathers, including the snow, to get to church on Sundays. While we lived at "Gayhurst" Belle Vue Road, I used to see her ride past sometimes. For years I remember she nursed her mother-in-law, who was bed ridden in an upstairs bedroom, until she died. Her mother-in-law had lived with them (Auntie Lily and Uncle Claude) at their house in Wivenhoe Road, Alresford, which is the next village to Wivenhoe. It was a rural property and they used to grow most of their own vegetables and flowers in their large garden.

Auntie Lily Wyatt

Margery Wyatt

Margery Wyatt: She married a man named Frank. They had children but I can't remember how many. I do know that, as a child, I used to visit now and again, when they moved into a house on the housing estate, where we lived at Old Heath, Colchester. I used to push one of the children or babies in the big high pram, that Mum had and walk around the estate with them. I remember going to visit, while pushing one of my younger brothers in the pram, to see their new baby, but we were not allowed to stay long as they were very house proud. I don't remember my mother and Auntie Margery ever visiting each other.

Winnifred Wyatt

Winnifred (Winnie) Wyatt: She married Jack Dodson and they had two children, a daughter, Daphne, and a son, John, who both married and had children. When she was younger my cousin, Daphne, woke up one night with pain in her eye, she had been bitten by some sort of fly and sadly had to lose the eye. However, she was very brave about it all and grew up to marry and have her own family.

My Grandmother-Nanna Tainton:
I have written a fair bit in the story of this special Nanna. She only had one child, who was my mother (Jessie Emily). Her maiden name was Davey. She had three brothers Bill, George and Mick, (whose real name was Christopher) Davey. Nanna was a widow for several years before marrying Arthur Tainton after the Second World War. (We called him Uncle Arthur not Granddad).

Bill: He was married and lived at Clacton-on-Sea. Essex. I am not sure how many children they had. I only remember visiting them a couple of times with Nanna. Uncle Bill just worked as far as I know during the tourist season on Clacton Pier. I am not sure what he did.

George: He married Elsie, Nanna's friend (recorded about Uncle George in the story).

Mick: His wife, Gladys, died when I was four and half years old, leaving him with two sons, Bobbie and Ronnie. He married again, to a German refugee named, Anne, she already had two children one, named Topsy, whom she brought to live with them and the other was a son who seems to have been left in Germany. Uncle Mick had two daughters by Anne they named them Jessie and Sylvia. All of Uncle Mick's children married and had children.

Ena Wyatt

Ena Wyatt: I don't remember Auntie Ena, I just know of her.

It was good to be able to walk down the village for shopping and sometimes call in to see the uncles and aunt's on the way there or back. Many times they could be standing in the front garden talking to the neighbours and it was nice to walk past just to say 'Hello' while pushing my own child along in her pram. I always think that village life is very special.

I hope this has given you a little idea of how some of my life has been.
Love & God Bless you from Jessie.

Jessies brothers and sisters

Cyril Wyatt

Christopher Wyatt

Clive and his daughter, Debbie Wyatt

Jasmine, Jill and Jessie

Jessie's sister, Jean and Pamela her daughter in law

A Prayer and a Psalm
I hope you like this special Prayer.

Dear God I pray that I may be filled
With Righteousness that comes through your
Son Jesus Christ. (Philippians: chapter 1 verse 11)
I pray that Jesus may be Lord of my life for ever and ever.

May I grow in your love God and be
Filled evermore with your holy Spirit,
Also with your fruits and gifts of The Holy Spirit.
That you may use me to help others.
I pray that I may be so filled with your love,
Peace and joy that it may emanate through me for others to see.

That they may come to know Jesus,
That He died for us on the cross.
I pray that my sins are forgiven,
- please God and help me to know when
You have forgiven me each time. - Please God,
So that I can feel that release in my Spirit
To do your will each day and for ever.

I pray that I never forget or take for granted
That Jesus died for my sins on the cross,
That only through Him am I saved.
Giving you my body for your Holy Spirit
To work through and use as a temple for you God.
May I ever know your saving grace and live in your Kingdom forever.
Amen.

Psalm: chapter 18 verse 11
He made darkness His Secret Place.
His canopy around Him was dark waters.
And thick Clouds of the Skies.

Yes, God does hide Himself from us as this part of the Psalm says. However, travelling home one day by plane, we were flying through the most beautiful clouds. The colours were incredible to see as the sun was going down. I believe that I was privileged to see the Glory of part of God's Universe. So this is what I wrote about it:-

You hide in the dark cloud the greatest treasure that ever could be.
Everlasting, Beautiful, so bright our eyes cannot see.
The beauty the glory the power and the joy.
The glorious brightness too bright for human eye.
No wonder you hide in the dark cloud God, veiled from our eyes.
You are so awesome, so beautiful so bright-you are eternal light.
Just a glimpse you let me see-it truly was too wonderful for me,
The colour was heavenly, so bright so pure.
No palette on earth could ever procure anything so bright with light and so, so, pure.
No wonder you hide in the dark cloud God,
To shield and protect us from your awesome power.
Yet you give us a yearning to know you more God.
We search for your Kingdom and look to the skies.
I praise you now that you protect our eyes from your brightness.
Your beautiful, your powerful light.
The light of the universe is there in the dark cloud,
When we come home to Heaven we will abound in your glorious, wonderful, effervescent light because our earthly bodies will be shed and our spirit bodies will be able to stand the brilliance,
The power, the wonder of you God our Heavenly Father.
We shall then see. The veil will be gone from our eyes,
The Dark Cloud, will hide us then from the world,
When we come into our Heavenly Home and see your incredible, eternal throne. We shall then see as we are now seen.

Jessie Larman is now a well known artist in Carnarvon. Examples of her outstanding work are pictured below showing a painting of an English country garden painted in 1973 before she emigrated to Australia and another showing a view of Carnarvon of the surge wall along West Street painted in 2008.

"Olde Worlde English Country Garden" by Jessie Larman 1973

"Surge Wall - West Street Carnarvon" by Jessie Larman 2008

www.ingramcontent.com/pod-product-compliance
Lightning Source LLC
Chambersburg PA
CBHW040322300426
44112CB00020B/2840